T0117013

YOU WRITE POETRY?
BE SERIOUS!

A Memorial to Gordon Frank Martin -
19th May 1950 - 13th April 2008

Gordon F Martin

iUniverse, Inc.
New York   Bloomington

YOU WRITE POETRY? BE SERIOUS!
A MEMORIAL TO GORDON FRANK MARTIN - 19TH MAY 1950 - 13TH APRIL 2008

iUniverse books may be ordered through booksellers or by contacting:

iUniverse
1663 Liberty Drive
Bloomington, IN 47403
www.iuniverse.com
1-800-Authors (1-800-288-4677)

Because of the dynamic nature of the Internet, any Web addresses or links contained in this book may have changed since publication and may no longer be valid. The views expressed in this work are solely those of the author and do not necessarily reflect the views of the publisher, and the publisher hereby disclaims any responsibility for them.

ISBN: 978-1-4401-3283-4 (sc)
ISBN: 978-1-4401-3284-1 (ebook)

Printed in the United States of America

iUniverse rev. date: 9/02/2009

Gordon Martin was my brother and my friend. Those of us who loved him have found it difficult to come to terms with his untimely death in spite of the fact that he was ill for such a long time. The compilation of this book of his written works has been an emotional but healing experience for me and is a memorial to him and to his indefatigable life.

Gordon was born, the youngest of three children, to Lily and Gordon Martin, on 19th May 1950. He spent a happy childhood in Whitwell, Derbyshire, the village of his birth where he and his elder brother Roy enjoyed the boyish pastimes of the day including football, which was to remain a life long passion. The death of Roy at the age of sixteen, during an asthma attack, had a profound effect on Gordon's young life.

The siblings attended Whitwell Infant and Junior schools and the boys later attended Staveley Grammar School. Leaving school at sixteen Gordon continued his education through day release and home study gaining qualifications in accountancy, which was to become his chosen career and during which time he married and had two sons,
David and Andrew.

At the age of thirty seven having worked his way up through several companies, to become Financial Director at Beezer Homes Yorkshire, a company with a twenty million pound turnover, and having met and married his wife Maureen, he was diagnosed with Parkinson's Disease.

Physically and mentally unable to continue such a demanding role he retired from work and with Maureen becoming his carer, their lives were changed irrevocably and forever.

However, he was unable to let himself stagnate and fought constantly to lead as normal a life as his illness would allow and it was at this time that he turned to one of his first loves, the written word. From this source springs this book.

This book is dedicated to the memory of two brothers
Roy and Gordon
Both very special, dearly loved and missed beyond words

The memory of their lives and struggles to lead a normal life in spite
of crippling illnesses is a daily inspiration

FORWORD

Gordon's death in April 2008 left a gaping hole in our lives which is impossible to fill. A man of tall stature, his personality was as big as he was and when he entered a room, even during his illness, he exuded a presence and commanded respect from everyone else there. He was our own "oracle" on any subject under the sun. If Gordon didn't know the answer then he knew how to find it, so inevitably he was the one to whom we always turned whatever the problem. His ready wit, unfailing cheerfulness, and the capacity to relate to each and every one of us in a loving and lovely way made him such a huge part of all our lives. He lived every day to its fullest capacity refusing to be cowed by the crippling effects of Parkinson's Disease.

It is hard to see any good come out of the devastating illness which robbed him of a normal life with his beloved wife Maureen and his two sons David and Andrew. It was however during that illness that his love of the written word and for poetry and prose was allowed to grow and expand in a way in which it might never have done had he continued his career in commerce and in particular in accountancy.

This book is Gordon's. It is life as he saw it and lived it. It felt impossible to edit his works, so they have all been included, a few with his own footnotes. Some of the verses are very personal, reflecting his own interests, loves, fears and at times confused thinking brought on by the effects of the drugs used to treat his Parkinson's. Others reflect his humour, general knowledge and interest in current affairs and always his command of the English language.

Enjoy what follows and celebrate the life of Gordon Martin.

GORDON PREFIXES HIS POETRY WITH A DEDICATION OF HIS OWN

I've done many things in my life
Some I'm even proud of
Some I wish I hadn't
Some - would it be that I could do them again
One thing is for sure
My parents were the best anyone could wish for
And my wife Maureen
Along with her sister Linda
Are up there as two of the
Finest people ever to walk this earth.
My sister and brother too
And my children David and Andrew
And finally Terry, Julia and Cathrine
Joy and Ian

This book is for them
So like it or hate it
Please treat it with respect
…..they at least deserve that

Gordon Martin 20/03/2007

Doing Different Things
© **Gordon martin** 1994

I
When I walk the city main street
People whisper and turn away
It's getting very hard to cope
Having nightmares at midday
I think it's time I made a stand
This oppression sticks and clings
You're saying what you used to say
But you're doing different things

2
Now I don't know about tangled love
Or remember that twist of fate
Nor care about the time I called
And watched you hesitate
But I know that I still love you
Please tell me that it isn't true
What they're saying on the grapevine
About me and him and you

3
Outside in the distance somewhere
You can hear a blackbird's sweet refrain
But inside this house of misery
Words intensify the pain
And I just keep getting nervous
Each time the telephone rings
You're saying what you used to say
But you're doing different things

4
After all these years together
I think it's time I made a move
We know each other now, so well
We've nothing left to prove

And I can't stand around and wait
While you take your time to choose
I want to stay here with you girl
But I'm frightened I will lose

5
So I'm filling up my suitcase
I've got a ticket in my hand
I'm walking down the corridor
Though little has yet been planned
And you're standing in the doorway
And you're fumbling with your rings
You're saying what you used to say
But you're doing different things

6
You look at me with tear filled eyes
That reach the bottom of my soul
And I look back and we both know
That we're paying too high a toll
So I put the suitcase on the ground
And I hold you close to me
I tell you that I love you still
And that's how it's going to be

7
Then you tell me that you love me
Say it was all inside my head
And you touch me like you want me
And resurrect me from the dead
Now I know that you still care for me
With a warmth only your love brings
You're saying what you used to say
And now you're doing the same things.

ONE HUNDRED DEGREES
© Gordon martin 1994

One hundred degrees and rising,
It's getting too hot to speak.
The devil's gone on holiday
To Iceland for a week,
And me I'm sitting here
Just hoping for a break,
Maureen's on the lounger.
How much sun can she take?
"I wish it would get warmer,
Then stay like that a month,
I could top my tan up every day,
Just take time off for my lunch...."
Me, I sit here lonesome,
Praying for respite,
And longing for the evening and
Coolness of the night.
But it's only my imagination
Of what summers might be had,
If we didn't live in England
And the weather wasn't bad
So I sit here writing poetry
And the wind just blows away,
Maureen reads her romance books,
Hoping tomorrow's a better day.

Parkinson's
© Gordon martin 1994

I am lying here in bed
My left hand is shaking
uncontrollably. My whole
body feels as if it doesn't
belong to me, it is just a dead
weight that I am attached to.
I am just a thinking mind,
clear, concise and intelligent ,
shackled by this immobile
prison called the human body.
The thing that has served me
so well for forty years now
seems likely that it will
become my enemy.

My mind is like the computer I
write this on. Capable of
consuming so much more
knowledge, open to ideas and
experiments not yet brought
to it, waiting for some new
sequence of events to thirst
the necessary programme of
variety needed to avoid
boredom and stagnation.

As I lie here I wonder what
use is it if I can't move. The
whole process of taking in any
knowledge seems pointless (l
stop typing for a moment and
try to adjust my posture as
although I have only been sat
at the keyboard ten minutes
both my legs have gone dead

and my back aches. I ease my
left leg forward with my right
hand. Thank God He left this
until the last and gave me time
to come to terms with my
Condition). I am in a crystal
clear frame of mind not the
doldrums I sometimes sink
into. The whole concept of
working, to me, is that it is
regular and repetitive. I do not
feel I am even now able to
qualify on either count, though
it seems some do and in
regard to them l admire them
most highly.

One of the main reasons I am
able to cope with this is that I
do not have to show myself to
the world when I am unwell. I
bask in my anonymity, safe in
the arms of invisibility, away
from the glare of attention
that no matter how helpful
friends are, just makes me
more aware that I have
changed from the buzzing,
probing, enquiring,
enthusiastic businessman that
I was. Transformed, like
Superman in reverse, into this
mind and body, now quite
separate, the latter acting as
an embedded anchor to the
former, the good ship Santa
Maria, still wanting to
discover America.

I read about Ray Kennedy
and how he needed a buggy
once to carry him to the
departure gate of an airport
and having got there found his
medication taking effect, able
to jump off and run up the
steps. I can totally identify
with that situation. Will I have
the courage to do the same
when my condition reaches
that point, which it
undoubtedly will.

I cannot imagine wanting to
do anything or go anywhere if
my condition deteriorates
significantly, but my
intelligence tells me that if I
want to be a part of the world I
love so much, my wife, my
family, my friends; and to do
the things I love to do - watch
sport, visit America (I love
America), drive, shop, compute,
then I must persevere and beat this.
The alternative is too awful to
consider.

So I am positive and fight on, I
gain much strength from
those close to me.
I hope that they realise how
much my heart feels for them,
people caring for me who
have no need to, who put their
own misfortunes to one side
to help, they are precious
beyond words.

And I am mobile.
The tablets are working.
I feel great.
Let's get the show on the road.
What's that you say, "wait for me?"
Come on, hurry up,
We're going to have some fun........

FRIENDS

© Gordon martin 1994

1
I can't think of a better plan
To pass the time away
Than to walk along Gulf Boulevard
At the closing of the day
To visit friends who live nearby
And take a drink or two
Or three or four or even more
I'm not counting, nor are you

2
We men talk about the government
Or about the president
Or about some other politician
With a declaration of intent
And the topics get more varied
As the clock ticks round to ten
But the women are much wiser
They just talk about the men

3
We switch the television on
To check the baseball score
The New York Mets and Blue Jays
Who are we rooting for?
The pretzels on the table
Are going faster than the Mets
The Blue Jays lead it five to zip
No-one's taking any bets

4
And we're really very settled
Our hosts are treating us so kind
We talk of where to go and what to do
Tomorrow, we don't mind

We're just happy to be in St. Pete's Beach
With good friends who stand the test
Nina and George, we'd like to say
We think that you're the best

5
And you make us very welcome
We'll come again for sure
Eat out at the Brown Derby
And walk along the shore
Get drunk around The Swigwam
Go shopping in the mall
The boys visit the "Ted Williams"
The girls hear the clothes shop call

6
Oh to be back in America
Relaxing by the pool
Taking time out for a cocktail
Swimming to keep cool
Instead it's autumn back in England
On a cold and rainy night
Honey ring the travel agent shop
And book us on a flight

7
Put me on that silver bird
Fly me across the sea
Sit me next to Nina and George
That's where I want to be
We'll laugh and joke 'til early morn
Of things done in the past
Of things we'll do in future
Be sure it's not the last

8
So fill the glasses to the brim
Fill them full of beer

And drink to friendship that we have
Good times, good friends, good cheer
Raise your glasses to the toast,
We've said before, and how:
"Same time, same place" we always say
"Thirty years from now."

FRIENDS (PART 2)

1
I wrote you a poem back in England
Well surprise surprise here's another
About a man for whom we have a great respect
And a woman that treats us like a mother

2
Get down in the easy chair
And take a well earned rest
No matter how far you travel this crazy world
The journey that takes you home is always the best

3
It's attitude adjustment time
Fill your glass until it overflows
And say cheers to Mo and Gordon Martin
And we'll do the same for Nina and George Primrose

In the garden at 10 Franklin Avenue
Dad, Roy, Gail and Mum with Gordon on her knee 1950

ORDINARY DAY

They're boarding the Titanic
The R101 is in the air
The Marie Celeste sails for Atlantis
Hitchcock's birds are everywhere
Dali's paintings fill 10 Downing Street
The taxman's playing Santa Clause
Flipper is circling Blackpool bay
Together with Moby Dick and Jaws
Godzilla and Pavarotti
Are seen at the rock show
England give Taylor his job back
Terry Venables has to go
Doncaster Rovers win the premier league
The national cricket team win at all
Spike Milligan wins the Booker prize
For his part in Hitler's downfall
Prince Charles decides to grow his hair long
Andre Agassi cuts his short
Hermes wants to visit Mercury
He's flying from the nearest airport
Gail and Alma's café is full of people
From other soaps of late
Sharon sits with Sinbad
Barry Grant's talking to Frank Tate
Devon Loch's just won the National
Mail says "the Sun's best for the news"
Lennox Lewis is set to fight King Kong
Major asks for Prescott's views
Norman Wisdom is the new James Bond
Wales play in a world cup
The banks are giving tenners away
Things are on the up and up
But when I ask my children
What's happened while I've been away
Nothing much, is all I get
It's been an ordinary day

Is There Life On Earth
© Gordon martin 1994

1
I go out walking with my wife
On deciding to take some air
We go down to the local shops
There'll be activity there
But upon arriving at the shops
Much to our dismay
A sign reads "closed - bank holiday,
Come back another day"
What's the point of having shops
If they're places you can't go
The only sane people in this place
Are me and my wife Mo

2
I decide to go and visit
My mother and father for the day
When I get there they start to tell me
What happened on holiday
How a day trip became a nightmare
When the driver stopped part way
And they had to climb a steep hill home
Great, when you're getting grey
I can't believe how people act
And don't know when to stop
The only sane people in this place
Are me and mom and pop

3
I've been paying my health charges
For twenty years or more
And now I've started claiming
I'm told they've shut the door
On recouping charges re my illness
Keep fit, don't say you're off it

15

Don't cause the fund to pay out
And take away their profit
They're more concerned with making bucks
Money greater, health care lesser
The only sane people in this world are
Me and the professor

4
I go down to the racecourse
I want to have a flutter
"I've got the winner of this race"
I overhear the next man mutter
He looks like he's been here before
So I take up his advice
And rush off to the tote hall
It looks a tempting price
The horse comes last and now I see
The tipster is a bookie
He's the only sane person at the course
Apart from me, and I'm, a rookie

5
I put on a police video
You can buy it from the shops
About some thieving bastard on the run
Escaping from the cops
Why don't they get all of the burglars
Murderers, rapists and lowlife
Put them all together
Give them all a knife
Let them rob and stab each other
Of course I hold a grudge
The only sane people left in here
Are me and the hanging judge

6
I go to watch the football match
It's such a joy to see

Man. United do the double
I'm as happy as can be
The Giants are getting better
Now that Handley's gone
The Blue Jays, world champs back to back
My teams are second to none
But can Alec keep his side together
We'll have to wait and see
The only sane people in the world
Are Eric Cantona and me

7
I switch the television on
A politician's there on view
He's telling us what's good for us
Can't he come up with something new
How can we take him serious
When another scandal breaks
He never gives straight answers
Or admits he made mistakes
The way he makes out if you vote
For him you're on a winner
The only crazy people in this world
Must be me and Dennis Skinner

YOU

1

I've never admired Gainsborough
His blue period made me blue
Or understood Picasso
I don't think he had a clue
His paintings don't make sense to me
But I've always admired you

2

I've never wanted to be well known
And put on public view
Or be seen in the right circles
Or make speeches all night through
The only thing I have to say
Is I want to be with you

3

I've never worshipped false gods,
Be they aged, be they new
And when you die you don't come back
Re-incarnation just won't do,
But of all the earthly pleasures
You know that I worship you

4

I've never been happy with people,
Who bite off more than they can chew
And take you for some kind of fool
Because they've nothing else to do
Don't they know that they're the losers
And I'm happy to be with you

5

I've never been to Bombay
Afghanistan or Timbuktu,
Or watched the midnight sun go down,
Or seen the northern lights shine through
I've never been to the ends of the earth
But let me always be with you

HOME FROM WORK
© **Gordon martin 1994**

There's a recidivist in the kitchen
He's taking all that he can get
And a mathematician in the bathroom
I haven't figured him out yet
In the bedroom an escapologist
He'll have to pay to come out
A town crier in the hallway
He's in with a bit of a shout
In the garden there's a misogynist
You can't say he's a ladies man
And the athlete in the dining room
Just looks like an also ran
The reprobate in the parlour
Seems as if he's going through hell
The lumberjack on the stairway
Sounds as though he might have fell
The pilot on the landing
Is looking rather plain
The madman in the cellar
Is acting quite insane
The lycanthropist at the doorway
Wolf whistles at the lasses
The optician moves from room to room
Collecting all the glasses
The joker on the telephone
I'm told is quite a card
The hypnotist looks so serious
I'll have to watch him hard
The ventriloquist isn't saying much
He's sitting there dumb struck
The librarian sat beside him
Has got his head stuck in a book
And when you get home from your labour
A cashier tells you loud
It's not every day you walk inside
And meet such an interesting crowd

19

UNTITLED

1
This is a piece of self indulgence
About some people that I'm proud to know
I hold them in the highest regard
But I don't want to put them on show

2
I want to keep them for myself
To hold council when ever I need aid
To show me the straight and narrow
And how the game is played

3
To be there when I need them
Which, of course, they always are
A beam to light the darkest path
Like the night sky's brightest star

4
There's always food on the table
A pillow to lay my head
All they ask is that I act pleasantly
Nothing more needs to be said

5
There's drink to quench the driest throat
And conversation and good heart
And they'd give their very life for me
Of them I'm such a part

6
By now you know the people
That these lines may give fame
You may not know them personally
But you must know two the same

7
And I'm very proud to put this down
In full and open face
And say to my parents, you're special
No-one could ever take your place

THAT'S ALL

Linda's an angel, Terry's sound,
A better family can't be found
Julia's smashing, Cathrine's ace
Four of the nicest people in the human race

Day out at Gunthorpe Bridge, Lincs,
Roy, Gail, Dad, Gordon (c 1956)

?

© **Gordon martin**

How can a flamingo stand on one leg
Has an overheated chicken ever laid a boiled egg
Has a robin ever been arrested for stealing a car
Has an eagle ever shot two under par

The Vagrant
© **Gordon martin 1994**

1
Sometimes when you're travelling
Along a dusty road
You come upon a vagrant
Bearing a heavy load
All his possessions carried
On his bending back
A black plastic bin liner
Used as a haversack
An overcoat about his frame
Even though the day is hot
Tied round the waist with parcel string
It's the best belt that he's got
His old black shoes are ripped around
The toe cap and above
Upon his hands he wears a pair
Of worn out fingerless gloves
His beard is rough and shabby
His hair uncombed and grey
He walks just like a confused crab
As he shuffles on his way
His teeth are in need of some repair
His cough deep from within
He hasn't eaten for three days
He spent what he had on gin

2
Do you think he once was married
Do you think he had a home
Perhaps he worked in farming
Or sailed the briny foam
Could he have met misfortune
Or did he choose this way of life
Has he had some pleasure in this time
Or is his history all strife

25

And whereabouts is he heading
From where did he appear
What keeps him motivated
Will he last another year
How will he cope with winter
When he's facing blinding snow
Will he find some quiet haven
Will he know just where to go
Did he once shoot pool for money
Did he play for a football team
Was he seen on the television
Does he hold inside a dream
That one day he'll be peaceful
And happy and content
Is he hoping for a better life
Do you think that's his intent

3
Sometimes when your travelling
Down a motorway that's new
An expensive car comes past you
And the driver is in view
He's smart and he's good looking
He's got gold upon his wrist
He wears expensive clothing
A deadline he's never missed
His smile can melt the iciest heart
A glance will make you dizzy
He's always been one step ahead
Both his hands are busy
And he's always talking to the girls
For that, time must be made
And buy them a drink or two
It's all expenses paid
He'll sweep them off their feet of course
The plan's already set
He knows exactly what will happen
He's never failed yet

He's mister indestructible
And mister wonderful too
He loves them and he leaves them
He's got some business to see to

4
Do you think that he is married
Do you think he has a home
Perhaps he works in banking
Travelling to Paris or Rome
Has he always been successful
Did he choose this way of life
Has he always found some pleasure
Has he even heard of strife
And whereabouts is he heading
From where did he appear
What keeps him motivated
Will he last another year
How will he cope with a market crash
Will it ruin him overnight
Will he need a cash injection
Will he have set the market price right
Did he once contest the Olympics
Did he ride the horse of the year show
Was he seen on the television
Winning the puissance at first go
Is he satisfied with what he's got
And happy and content
Is he hoping for a better life
Do you think that's his intent

5
Sometimes when your travelling
Along the avenue
Do you ever notice
Someone looking across at
You ?...............................

No Good
© Gordon martin

1

I was looking for assistance
I was in a tight spot
I was getting badly beaten
I'd given it everything I'd got

2

All I needed was some respite
From the pounding I was taking
Someone to soothe my wounds for me
And stop my body aching

3

And I thought you'd be that person
After all, I'd helped you make the break
And so I came to you for comfort
Was that a big mistake

4

You were even worse than useless
You didn't even make a start
At patching up the wounds and scars
Or mending the broken heart

5

But I guess I should have known better
After all I had a clue
When I came to you for refuge
And you had something better to do

6

So don't worry you can't help me
I won't bother you no more
I won't ring you on the telephone
Or come knocking at your door

7
And I don't care if I never see you
For eternity and a day
In fact if I see you coming
I'll just walk the other way

8
I'd rather be a loner
Sat with nothing left to do
Than have material things around me
That come with company like you

9
And now you know just how I feel
I suppose it's understood
But I've got to say it to you once
I think that you're no good

HOPE FOR ME
©Gordon martin 1994

1

I found out only yesterday
The truth about your meddling
That you were making lots of money
From the drugs that you were peddling
But I know you'll never realise
The necessity to be free
Until they lock you up in jail
And throw away the key
At least I'll have one problem less to sort out
And there'll be some hope for me

2

An old friend told me that he's thinking
Of taking a vacation
He says he's getting tired
And his body won't stop aching
I guess he didn't stop to think
The reason that he's flagging
Is because he leads a double life
He's even started bragging
Maybe he'll take a trip and not come back
Then I'll get a break from his nagging

3

I went to see the gypsy
At the in town travelling fair
I hoped I might succeed at last
And get some better advice there
But the gypsy was just a crazy
I didn't stay long, it's true
She wanted paying twenty pounds
For something I already knew
That someone close to me is leaving
I just hope it isn't you

4

I'm getting calls most every day
And letters all the time
From charities wanting donations
Please put your money on the line
A pound for the donkeys in distress
Send to Greenpeace in the mail
More money for the world wildlife fund
A tenner to save the whale
But try borrowing from an orang-utan
And I guarantee you'll fail

5

Now all these tales that I relate
Are mostly stuff and nonsense
But here and there's a piercing thought
With deep meaning and much relevance
All I ask you reader to consider
And deduce with a detective's art
Which of it is nonsense
And which the meaningful part
Enjoy the nonsense have a laugh
But take the other to your heart

6

Then perhaps you'll start to understand
The confusion that sometimes races
Around and around inside my head
And why I've many different faces
The conundrum that I see I am
And know I'll always be
Sometimes bound and troubled
Other times easy and carefree
And come to see that comprehension
Gives hope to you and me

My Life As A Sports Almanac
Part One 1950 - 9
© Gordon martin 1994

1950
America beats England by a goal
The U.S Open is Hogan's last hole
Wales grand slam season comes alive
Yankees take the second of five

1951
Piggott is a winner at twelve
Marciano puts Louis on the shelf
May gets a 100 on his England start
Fangio takes the motor racing world apart

1952
Man United beat Arsenal 6-1 to finish top
Little Mo Connolly is Wimbledon's cream of the crop
Zatopek runs for Olympic golds three
Surrey win first of seven to be

1953
Matthews casts his magic spell
Sir Gordon and Pinza give the others hell
England's lions finally lose a home game
Puskas makes them look so tame

1954
Bannister breaks the 4 minute mile
Jaroslav Drobney takes Wimbledon in style
Piggott's Derby on Never Say Die
West Germany on a world cup high

1955
83 dead at the Le Mans 24
Bobet wins his third cycling tour
Campbell breaks 200 miles per hour
Brooklyn Dodgers above all others tower

1956
Devon Loch falls for no apparent reason
Floodlight football is in its first season
Yankees' Larsen pitches the only world series perfect game
Marciano retires, the only undefeated heavyweight you can name

1957
Huddersfield lead Charlton 5 - 1 who are down to ten men
Summers scores 3 in 6 minutes, then again and again
Huddersfield equalise in the 88th minute
But Summers puts Ryan in, 7-6 Charlton win it.

1958
Munich Air Disaster for Man U
UEFA in sympathy say enter next year too
Can you believe the Football League fools
Declined because it was "against the rules"

1959
Shankley set the task of building Liverpool up
When they lose 2-1 to Worcester in the Cup
Nottingham Forest with Tooting and Mitcham draw
Then go on to win the trophy, 2-1 the score

GUESS WHO?
© **Gordon martin 1994**

He's a younger version
Of a very amiable man
He's reasonably good looking
He's a Man United fan
He supports the second best team
In America you can see
I think they're called the Dolphins
And Marino is the key
He's always got a smile for you
And he's helpful, it's got to be said
That is unless it's morning
He's always fast asleep in bed
He likes a Friday night out
Drinking more and more
Now where have I heard that said
And who about, before?
We have the crack together
About sport and life and such
I think I'm teaching him the ropes
He thinks I'm talking far too much

LAST VERSE PARENT VERSION

But it's all good natured cut and thrust
And when all is said and done
You'd expect the father to be a little
Smarter than the son

LAST VERSE SON VERSION

But it's all good natured cut and thrust
If it keeps him happy I'd rather
Pretend he's smarter than I am
After all, he is my father

GUESS WHO?
II
© **Gordon martin**

Don't you know by now how much I care
Can't you see it in my eyes
Don't you realize I've seen too much of life
To be taken by surprise

No matter what the situation
You'll always be in my head and heart
And I'll always be wishing you the best
No matter how far we are apart

You see you'll always be special to me
After all you're my firstborn son
Make the most of your life ahead
This is it, it can't be re-run

And sometime in the future
A son might be part of your plan
And then you may, like I did with my father,
Comprehend why he made me into a man

Scout BBQ c 1958 - Gordon front right

Day trip to Skegness
Gordon, Roy, Granddad, Dad, Grandma, Mum c.1961

ME AND YOU

1
I've considered many things of late
About our lives together
The years that lay behind us
And the future that's forever
And I come to see as I reflect
The truth of our connection
When we're happy we could beat the world
When we're not we face rejection

2
We talk about our plans and schemes
And what the future holds
Where we see ourselves ten years from now
How the mystery unfolds
But though we try to control it
Life is full of fateful turns
When we're happy we could beat the world
When we argue it just burns

3
And so we learn to take each day
Without premeditation
And if we learn more of ourselves
It's been a worthwhile education
Be understanding, consider others
And pause before complaining
When we're happy we could beat the world
When we're not our life blood's draining

4
So on we go, forever on
Down life's path, we can't turn back
What's past is past, we can't undo
The things that turned out black

I'll try and be as wise as my father
You just be the same as your mother
We'll be happy, and we'll beat the world
If we're not we'll destroy each other

4

(Alternative last verse)
So on we go, forever on
Down life's path we can't turn back
What's done is done and will always be
White ever white and black ever black
We take the challenge that life is
Mistakes forgiven regrets denied
Knowing that together we are stronger
And build on hope and love and pride

I'VE GOT THEM PARKINSON CAN'T MOVE, CAN'T SMILE CAN'T STOP SHAKING BLUES

© Gordon martin 1994

1
The lads are doing twenty questions at the Flarepath Thursday quiz
Dylan's singing "someone's got it in for me"
I guess that's how it is
Maureen's in the bedroom
Catching up on the soap show news
I've got them Parkinson can't move can't smile, can't stop shaking blues.

2
Andrew's off to see United
Gail's making plans for Tenerife
If she ever gets Derek to stay there
It'll be a great relief
Robert Palmer sings a song
Like me he's "looking for clues"
I've got them Parkinson can't move can't smile, can't stop shaking blues.

3
Dad's down at the bookies
I think he'll hit the jackpot yet
Mum talks about Australia
And the family she's not met
Elvis says "you can do anything
But lay off my blue suede shoes"
I've got them Parkinson can't move can't smile, can't stop shaking blues.

4
David's going through his collection checking a price or spotting a trend
Paul Simon sings of loneliness
"hello darkness my old friend"
Joy's up in Newcastle somewhere
Consuming quantities of booze
I've got them Parkinson can't move can't smile, can't stop shaking blues.

5
Ian must be down in Nottingham
He's got a degree in engineering -
Engineering some time with the girls
He presses on regardless and unfearing
ELO flood the room with sound
"they say someday your gonna lose"
I've got them Parkinson can't move can't smile, can't stop shaking blues.

6
Linda and Terry are at the Holly Bush
They're playing local league darts
"I'm turning Japanese" sing the Vapours
From the 1980's charts
Next it's Scott Walker's choice "There's no regrets"
What a good C.D. to choose
I've got them Parkinson can't move can't smile, can't stop shaking blues

The House On The Cataluna Road

© Gordon martin 1996

1

There's a white house on a hillside
There's a woman cherishes it with pride
There's a love that longs to be there
There's a heart pounding deep inside.

2

There's a courtyard cool and private
There's a kitchen clean and neat
There's a bedroom where two lovers laid
There's a dream almost complete

3

Put the woman in the hillside home
Let her tend it with love and care
And there enjoy your halcyon days
In a world you both can share

4

As the evening sun drops over the sea
And you look out at the beautiful scene
Think, is there any more idyllic place
That you have ever seen?

5

Let your heart find its true utopia
And your mind accept the golden dream
Let you soul find true contentment
Be happy – be the perfect team.

6

And though you've no name for this place yet
Don't let that ever be a load
Just call it *"CASA EN CALLE CATALUNA"*
The house on the Cataluna road

****

Note

Gordon's anthem to our lovely home in Tenerife

****

Different People, Same Pain
©Gordon martin 1994

1
He:
I can't understand why you don't know that whatever you state
will come to pass, the control you have over me is so great
even when I try to put up some kind of resistance
your relentless driving is gathering momentum in the distance.

2
She:
Just like the irresistible force takes all in its projection
your determination grinds and dissipates any objection.
Perhaps you understand your process of determination
or perhaps its just coincidental accidental extermination

3
She
I nearly left you yesterday but like every other time
I finished up resenting myself for putting our relationship on the line
I never even questioned why I consider materialistic possessions
more important than consuming relationship obsessions

4
He:
Surely lovers live to act out their idealistic suppositions
not to find that being together creates futile oppositions
but then those visions of you went around in my head
and once again I found myself deciding it was better left unsaid

5
He:
People on the fringe of an argument that's ice cool
are like driftwood about to be consumed by the whirlpool
they'll be gathered into the debate regardless of their involvement
in the overall confusion of this futile and pointless argument

6
She:
After all we know that the process is already started
by the very fact that you're talking to me and I've not departed
and the conclusion will become self evident and crystal clear
when we've punished each other enough and wiped the last tear

7
She:
Whatever the price we'd always pay it if an emotion we could steal or
borrow
but the cost cannot be simply measured as joy or sorrow
it's more concerned with an integrated process of continuation
of accumulating actions and the need for self determination

8
He
We have to believe that our destiny is determinable by our own
decisions
and in no way controlled by others' interference or derision
We concur with opinions that soak into the sponge of our conscience
and don't conflict with ideals or destroy any confidence

9
Both:
And I for my part must be content and simplistic
and reflective and placid and in no way vindictive

The Pub
© **Gordon martin 1994**

1
The landlord opens up the doors
for another night of drinking
it's wintertime in London town
and the fog is already sinking

2
Minutes later a man walks in
he's carrying a briefcase
he's dressed smart and he's clean shaven
and he looks around the place

3
He goes up to the bar and orders
a bottle of ice cold beer
he sits down at the corner stool
it's convenient and near

4
Soon a few of the regulars
make their way inside
"I don't think we'll be late tonight"
a man says to the female by his side

5
They're just two lovers out for a drink
they're happy to be together
soon they'll be holding each other close
as they walk home in the misty weather

6
Opposite them, beside the bandit
sits an old lady, in contemplation,
of how she can get about again
since her hip replacement operation

7
She smiles, she's full of mischief,
"I'll get that new hat and go walking,
I'll go striding down the street again
It'll set the neighbours talking"

8
There's a couple of young Australians
they've backpacked it all the way
one's missing home, he's going back
the other's here to stay

9
So tonight they're having a farewell drink
They've travelled far and wide and
they know that when they come to part
there'll be an emptiness inside

10
It's Thursday night and blow out time
for the girls by the picture wall
later they're off to the nightclub
they're going to have a ball

11
There'll be no stopping them tonight
it's fun they want to see
they've done their work, it's hair down time
who will the lucky lads be?

12
Some tourists and some theatre goers
some people down for the cup
A market trader, a flower seller
All help to fill the happy place up

13
Now the first man finishes his ice cold beer
and is gone in the swirling grey

"Hey, you've forgotten your briefcase"
the barman starts to say

14
They are the last words he ever speaks
as the briefcase explodes with a roar
and blinding flash of searing heat
and the pub and its patrons are no more

15
Another tragedy hits the news stands
the headline reads "Pub bombing - 50 dead"
but the ending of the story
will never, in the news, be read

16
In another part of London town
a man rushes across a street
he's dressed smart and he's clean shaven
and his night's work is complete

17
There's a lorry moving furniture
turning in the very same road
the driver's eager to get finished
when he delivers this last load

18
In the fog he never saw him
at least it partly evened up the score
it's just a pity that it didn't happen
some three or four hours before

19
So for all the innocent people
Let this story's message tell
To all the indiscriminate terrorists
May you burn and rot in hell

Back garden at home, Roy, Gordon and Lassie, c.1962

Taken one week before Roy's death in 1963
Barry, Gail, Roy, Dad, Mum and
Gordon with Lassie middle front

The End Of The World

How would the newspaper headlines be rendered
If they could be published the day after the world ended?

"FEAR AND TERROR FOR EACH REPROBATE"
"DISEASE AND PESTILENCE FOR EACH BIGGOT"

No

"THE FOUR HORSEMEN OF THE APOCALYPSE
BEATEN IN A PHOTO BY LESTER PIGGOTT"

To Whom It May Concern
© **Gordon martin 1994**

1
Your name brings back poignant memories
Of when we worked at the same firm
How you never stopped your gossiping
Even when it wasn't your turn

2
How you criticised my judgement
And left my pride badly bruised
And how I'll always remember you
For the yard and a half of tongue you never used

3
You could talk the back legs off a donkey
You could make a lion cower away
Your incessant drone drove us all mad
It was twenty four hours a day

4
You had a degree in ear bending
And a diploma in telling tales
Even the world's greatest orators
Would have the wind knocked out of their sails

5
And when you die and go to heaven
There will be arranged by the Holy Ghost
Headphones for God and Jesus
And cotton wool for the angelic host

THE DAY I MET YOU
© Gordon martin 1994

1
You were working on an oil rig
you were the toughest in the team
when the others felt like quitting
you were getting up a head of steam

2
I watched you board the helicopter
with a hundredweight bag on your back
you had muscles on your muscles
you'd never been known to crack

3
Superman came to you for advice
Popeye floundered in your shade
you got your shoes from the boatyard
your clothes were specially made

4
You had tattoos down both your arms
A tiger across your chest
that roared in anger when you flexed your muscles
when you boxed it was no contest

5
You were everything a man should be
Tall, dark, handsome and strong
But it's over, I can't see you again
Goodbye Penelope, so long

I'M HAPPY TO BE ALONE
© Gordon martin 1994

1
It's a empty sort of feeling
Brought on by loneliness
But when you're wanting peace and solitude
It's inevitable I guess
Quietness roars inside your head
Stillness moves around
Hunger feeds on your appetite
For the isolation you have found

2
An introspective review takes place
As you consider what is real
Are friends concerned with your concerns
Do they sense the way you feel
Do they read what's printed in the news
And reflect on it with sorrow
About what's happening to the world today
And where it's going tomorrow

3
When the headline making story reads
"A foetus can feel pain"
"1 had sex with mother and two daughters"
"War in Bosnia breaks out again"
"Maradona sent home after positive test"
"Colombian own goal scorer shot dead"
"National rail strike to continue"
What is there left to be said

4
What happened to the days gone by
When we avoided this onslaught
Of divisive and depressing news
And easy reading was all we bought

We have a vote, we use it
To install people, who want the chance
To sort out national problems
Not to make a song and dance

5

Let the doctors decide how pain is defined
They study for long enough
If they want my advice on the subject
They won't get it, isn't life tough
Don't hit me with another scandal
About a politician and his sex life
Who's bothered who he's with tonight
Leave the retribution to his wife

6

Why are we always surprised by war
It's obvious you must concede
There will always be fighting and destruction
While the world is ruled by greed
While ever there's one man alive
With power as his ambition sole
Through mock religion or the iron fist
Economics or thought control

7

To the politicians let me say
Get on with the job you're paid for
Stop getting side-tracked with irrelevancies
Don't come calling at my door
You've got the job you wanted
Go ahead and see it through
Leave me to enjoy my leisure time
And I won't bother you

8

What has happened in the world of sport
It was meant to be relaxing

Not played by junkies high on dope
Onerous and taxing
Where winning becomes everything
Why can't we take a step back
To when you stood with the opposition
And enjoyed the verbal crack

9
And the unions are back at their old tricks
Can't they get it in their mind
That by inconveniencing the ordinary guy
They only hurting their own kind
Leave me to my solitude
Is the position I've resolved
I'll put up with this empty feeling
It's better than being involved

SERENITY

1
I sit and watch people walk the vales
It's a pleasant summer night
There's much calm and easiness out there
No one has any need to care
In the golden brown twilight

2
What a beautiful world that stretches out
And over to the distant horizon
A thousand shades of greenery
Form nature's natural scenery
What pleasure to feast our eyes on

3
It's such a peaceful time of day
You feel the whole world healing
A harmonious song thrush sings a song
Water in an icy brook flows along
Such a relaxed and restful feeling

4
What beauty there is in simplicity
And in the natural order found
What peace there is in quietness
Like innocence free from all duress
When serenity does abound

MYSTERY ISLAND
© Gordon martin 1994

1
Darkness falls on Mystery Island
Where no soul can survive
Where everything is evil
And nothing leaves alive

2
The ghouls arise, the phantoms wail
Down by the waterside
Sea serpents swim around the hull
As the devil waits for the tide

3
The ghostly craft is leaving dock
The demon ship sets sail
The crew are not of human born
They're all so cold and pale

4
Their bones are skeleton networks
Pallid skin is stretched around
No muscle drives these spectres on
From hell their energy found

5
And off to sea the motley crew
Moves with relentless motion
A ghostly ship sails through the night
Upon a misty ocean

6
They work like demons to drive the ship
So hard, their bones a cracking
As they toil in deadly misery
Not one spectre to be found lacking

7
Their presence makes the water freeze
The temperature is falling
Up in the crow's nest, a banshee cries
"I sight the ship!" he's calling

8
And the crew look over to the place
His bony hand is waving
They spy the ship with staring eyes
Tonight there'll be no saving

9
The ship that sailed with good intent
Is caught in Satan's scheming
Drawn ever in by a ghostly aura
Its passengers asleep and dreaming

10
But when they wake from pleasant dreams
They'll not be able to cope
With the nightmare that's confronting them
And their lack of any hope

11
The seas grow colder by the minute
"Is that an iceberg?" the Captain's thinking
Too late to think wretched Captain, now
The Titanic has started sinking

12
So heed this story I relate
If upon the sea you float
Don't rise at night and look out to sea
Lest you see the evil boat

13
And spare a thought for the souls that died
On that icy night alone
Do they rest in peace with the good lord God
Or on Mystery Island moan

DEADLIER THAN THE MALE
© **Gordon martin** 1994

1
You think that it's a man's world
And that he's the master of his fate
Well listen to me brother
And take heed before it's too late
You think that man can pick and choose
There's no way he will fail
Just remember the female of the species
Is more deadly than the male

2
Philip the Handsome, the King of Castile
Was wedded to Joanna the Mad
And thereafter lived a life of regret
It's pitiful and sad
That such a good looking man as he
Lived a life to no avail
Just remember the female of the species
Is more deadly than the male

3
The French rebelled for equality and liberty
In brotherhood took up the fight
But Madam Guillotine took many
In France's darkest night
The notorious lady helped many
Step over death's dark veil
Just remember the female of the species
Is more deadly than the male

4
"We are stepped in blood so far
Returning were as tedious as go o'er"
The Scottish lord heard his lady say
As he paced the castle floor

And Lady Macbeth once again
Put her plans back on the rail
Just remember the female of the species
Is more deadly than the male

5
Pandora couldn't resist a look
She had to open the box and see
And in that moment of complete madness
Set all the world's troubles free
She must have regretted it instantly
As she became distraught and pale
Just remember the female of the species
Is more deadly than the male

6
The face that launched a thousand ships
Is a story to amaze
It's true that Helen of Troy's beauty
Left Paris in a daze
But were those sailors ever told
As the ships prepared to sail
Just remember the female of the species
Is more deadly than the male

7
So if you ever think that you can
Pull wool over the eyes
Of the one you love, desire or dream of
Be prepared for a big surprise
They've probably already been there
Done it, and had fun along the trail
Just remember the female of the species
Is more deadly than the male

On Franklin Avenue
Gordon on Dad's moped with Lassie c.1965

Dad, Gail, Mum and Gordon c.1983

24 Hours In 162 Words
© Gordon martin 1994

Get up
Have a shower
Get dressed
Electric power
Shave your face
Brush your teeth
Eat toast
Prepare to leave
Kiss wife
Shut the door
Drive car
Weather's poor
Wipers on
Heater too
Crazy kid
Passes you
Let him go
Thinks he is
Nigel Mansell
Indianapolis
Down the road
In the dike
Missed the corner
Get a bike
Get to work
Do a deal
Got a bargain
What a steal
Lunch time
Meet the boys
In the pub
Lots of noise
Talking sport
Fix a day
Man United

Leeds away
Back to work
Board Meeting
New Director
Warm greeting
Seems fine
Wait and see
Meeting over
Cup of tea
Home again
News reviewed
Dining out
Italian food
Minestrone
Penne Pasta
Orvieto
Cassata after
Quick swallow
Of cappuccino
To the concert
Julio
Of all the girls
Goes the song
Ladies love him
Can't do wrong
Nice Guy
Even so
Concert ends
Off we go
Back home
Bed's cosy
What next
Don't be nosy!

Are You Sure?

© Gordon martin 1994

1
Confidence is a blessing when it leads to success
But self-opinionated beliefs are the worst form of excess
To believe your own view is the one worthwhile solution
Is a damning indictment, a free speech dilution

2
If you think that it's fair to lay on others your views
why don't they have the same right with you if they choose

3
Why should any one person think that they know best
To such a degree that they can't stand the test
Of lucid argument and concise debating
Of alternative views someone else is relating

4
And you must be the only person alive
Who, without thought provocation, believes your mind will survive

5
If you can't stand to listen to a verbal oration
Of someone who tries to give reasoned persuasion
You must be so sure that your view is as certain
As one day you'll pass through death's dark final curtain

6
People are people, they will get their say
Or eventually stop trying and just walk away

THE ONE THOUSAND AND FIRST THING TO DO WITH A CUCUMBER

© Gordon martin 1994

1
We're an economic union whatever that phrase means
We get cheaper Brussels sprouts
Spanish onions and French beans

2
The Eurocrats, I read, have now discussed a new dictate
And arrived at the mind blowing conclusion
A cucumber can't be straight

3
Has anyone got the time of day to get me their telephone number
I'll tell them to stop wasting our cash
And what to do with their …agricultural policy

When Did You Stop Loving Me?

1
When did you stop loving me
Was it recent or long ago
How is it that as your woman
I'll be the last to know

2
When did you stop loving me
Can the balance be redressed
Can you talk in open honesty
Will our love survive the test

3
When did you stop loving me
Was it when I hurt your pride
Did it change the way you saw me
Were you bitter deep inside

4
When did you stop loving me
Was it when you said I'd changed
Did you start to rearrange your life
Was that when you became estranged

5
When did you stop loving me
Why can't you just come clean
Instead of making out it's fine
And avoiding awkward scenes

6
When did you stop loving me
Can you tell me and be true
Have you fallen out of love with me
Or has someone fallen in love with you

7
When did you stop loving me
Have you been unfaithful too
Is she just a friend, an old flame,
Or is she someone new

8
When did you stop loving me
Was it an accident so absurd
Or were you so overcome by stress
You couldn't have even cared

9
When did you stop loving me
Did you meet up simply and by chance
Or did you arrange it at the nightclub
When you asked her for a dance

10
When did you stop loving me
Was it when you went away
Did you meet someone who told you
It didn't have to be that way

11
When did you stop loving me
Did someone make a good connection
When you took the holiday you needed
Did you get some warm affection

12
When did you stop loving me
Why did you not come through
When temptation stood before you
Leave, was all you had to do

13
When did you stop loving me
And stay with her a day or two
I said I'd never cheat on you
I thought you said it too

14
When did you stop loving me
You know there's nothing smart
Pretending you still care for me
But reject me in your heart

15
When did you stop loving me
Others know so why can't I
Or is what you've always said to me
That you put me first, a lie

16
When did you stop loving me
Come on tell me if you can
Stop acting like an idiot
Start acting like a man

17
When did you stop loving me
Put your emotions out on show
Say what you've avoided saying
Then just pack your bags and Go

Why Is It?
© Gordon martin 1994

1
Why is it when you're late out
the bus has always gone
But when it's snowing, hail or rain
you wait forever and a day for one

2
Why is it when you're early for an appointment
the other party is always late
But when you get there after time
you're told "now you'll have to wait"

3
Why is it when you take a train
and find an empty seat
The person that sits next to you
is the most obnoxious you could meet

4
Why is it when you're not buying
the shops have got the size and colour
But when you're in a hurry
it's "no sorry but we've got about every other"

5
Why is it that the car park machines
don't take the coins in your purse
Or don't give change for pound coins
which is robbery at its worst

6
Why is it when you've waited all year
for that very special date
At five to five the boss comes in
and asks you to work late

7
Why is it that you always
choose the slowest supermarket queue
And when they open up another line
five get there in front of you

8
Why is it when you're expecting a call from
someone that makes you bubble
You hear a ring, rush to the phone
and get a load of trouble

9
Why is it that when you rest at last
from your day of toil and labour
The first thing that happens when it's quiet at last
is a visit from a neighbour

JUDGEMENT DAY
© **Gordon martin 1994**

1
There's a rumbling in the distance
and a stillness in the air
a hollow echoing eerie sensation
chaos and panic everywhere
Radio station broadcasts only crackle
confusion in every town and city
people run around in circles
wailing in self pity

2
Great tidal waves are pounding
over each river, sea and ocean
friends look at each other in stunned disbelief
they haven't got a notion
The air is hot and angry aircraft are melting in mid-air
earthquakes open up the ground
and buildings that stood majestic
are suddenly not there

3
The Pope is in a panic
The President doesn't have a clue
Ayatollahs look to each other for help
The Dali Lama doesn't know what to do
The Russians think it's a conspiracy
The Chinese think it's all been planned
The Libyans want to know whose side to take
There's debate in every land

4
Meteorites hit the earth consistently
there are equatorial forest rainstorms
the deserts are getting colder
ice on the cacti forms

The polar caps are melting
ships collide at sea
everywhere there's total destruction
desolation and debris

5
The power of the H-bomb
fades into insignificance
as the power of the Almighty
peels back any shred of resistance
Judgement Day, should it come to pass,
then this is how it might be related
so hope God doesn't tire of human folly
and destroy what He created

Gordon with sons David and Andrew, Lake District c.1984

APOCALYPSE FOREVER

© **Gordon martin 1994**

Armageddon finally happened
so everyone's in paradise
have passed from mortal toil and troubles
to an everlasting heavenly life
but on reaching heaven's pearly gates
they find before St Peter lets them stay
they're judged for the way they lived their lives
and if they lived in a righteous upright way
to the left a lift ascends to glory
the other sends all the sinners down
people from all walks of life
from paupers to teachers to kings in crowns
one man still believed he could slip the net
and avoid a future of eternal doom
but you can't escape, so you sit and wait
for your turn, in the purgatory room
Mussolini's black shirts - the Camere Rouge
- the Japanese torturers from World War 2
and the Gestapo all had the same decision
as the leaders of the Spanish Inquisition
Joan of Arc, Margaret Thatcher, and Saddam Hussein
aren't leaders here they all get treated the same
but they still get their chance to have their say
and they're all being sent a different way
one gets to heaven, one screams and shouts
one has to wait as the jury's still out
for the honest clean living and faultless man
is as rare as Eskimo on the streets of Iran
and the sins of the world are as light as a feather
to the One who instigated apocalypse forever

****

Note:
who knows?
like advice, we are able to relate
right and wrong to anyone...
so why do we seek it from others?

****

APOCALYPSE FOREVER

(alternative version)
© Gordon martin

Armageddon finally happened so everyone is here
all waiting to be judged at the final frontier
the lift to the left sends the sinners down
there are paupers in rags and kings in crowns
and who is that leading the next group away
he looks just like Robert Maxwell what can I say
and over to the right near the lift that ascends
are a group of Mirror pensioners and some of their friends
one suicide jockey tried a different route
with his dark sunglasses and Italian suit
so we won't be witness to his claim to doom
as we sit and wait in the purgatory room
There's a few arrived seemingly got mistaken
Shouldn't be in here so they're being taken
by the Holy Ghost to the Buffalo Tomb
as the Sioux and Apache call the reincarnation room
Mussolini's black shirts, the Camere Rouge,
the Japanese torturers from World War 2
and the Gestapo wait with the Spanish Inquisition
now that's got to be St Peter's easiest decision
Joan of Arc, Margaret Thatcher, and Saddam Hussein
not leaders here they are all treated the same
but they still get their chance to have their say
and they're all being sent a different way
and the honest clean living and faultless man
is as rare as Eskimo on the streets of Iran
and the sins of the world are as light as a feather
to the One who instigated apocalypse forever

2152

© Gordon martin 1994

2, 15, 2
4, 25, 12, 1, 14.
words written like da Vinci paints
eclectic literature for sure

2, 15, 2
4, 25, 12, 1, 14.
when you wrote Every Grain of Sand
you wrote the masterpiece searched for

2, 15, 2
4, 25, 12, 1, 14.
Robert Zimmerman the poet
I'm glad I listened at your door

****

Note:
love him hate him let him be
the maestro gives much pleasure to me
****

A Month's Food

1
It's a dark and desolate night out there
and there's a cold chill in the wind
Everyone that's on the streets tonight
is going to, or has already sinned.

2
The violence in the tenement blocks
is upstaged only by corruption on the street
A deal is struck in a darkened alleyway
and the contract is complete

3
The price is set, a life, a life
an innocent to the slaughter
A syringe full, a needle blunt,
and a father has lost a daughter

4
A man has made a hundred bucks
but in taking the devil's payroll
Money that wouldn't buy a month's food
has cost his eternal soul

****

Note
does anyone really believe drugs are O.K

****

.

AT THE BACK OF THE CROWD
© Gordon martin

1916

It's a rainy day in a Belgian poppy field
and man's stupidity is about to reach a new height
countless soldiers die for a square mile of land
for the folly of the few the masses fight
And standing alone at the back of the crowd
is a man with a cloak and a scythe and a burial shroud

1943

It's a clear day in a north German town
but soon the air will be filled with smoke
millions are dying day after day
without a prayer for their souls being spoke
And standing alone at the back of the crowd
is a man with a cloak and a scythe and a burial shroud

1963

It's a sunny day in a Texan town
street after street completely full
somewhere above a trigger clicks
A bullet in the president's skull
And standing alone at the back of the crowd
is a man with a cloak and a scythe and a burial shroud

33

It's a hot day in a middle eastern town
but soon the sun will be in eclipse
they're nailing an innocent to the cross
He wants water for His parched and burning lips
And standing alone at the back of the crowd
is a man with a cloak and a scythe and a burial shroud

????

It's a strange day in some undefined town
May be dry, sun, rain or mist
suddenly it happens and
the person you were no longer exists
And standing alone at the back of the crowd
is a man with a cloak and a scythe and a burial shroud

Life Everlasting

It's a beautiful day there's no need for towns
or angels in robes, or flowing white gowns
just peace and contentment and eternally bliss
brought here by the Man betrayed by a kiss
And standing unnoticed at the back of the crowd
watching over His own is **THE MASTER** *unbowed*

Barbed Wire
© Gordon martin

1

NO MATTER HOW BLACK THE CLOUD
NO MATTER HOW BARBED THE WIRE
NO MATTER HOW TALL THE FENCE
THEY CAN'T MATCH THE SUN'S FIRE

2
SO LET YOUR LOVE LIVE LIKE THE SUN
BURN AWAY THE BLACK CLOUD OF DOUBT
AND HOWEVER HIGH THE FENCE IS
IT CAN'T BLOCK YOUR LOVE OUT

3
AND HOWEVER DEEP AND DESTRUCTIVE
AND CUTTING THE WIRE
IT WILL MELT IN EXPOSURE
OF LOVE'S BURNING FIRE

A Chicago Bulls Basketball Hat
© Gordon martin

1
There's a guy just been on TV
from Chechnya or thereabouts
he's a freedom fighter for his people
he's handing guns and bullets out
He says his people are starving
no food and things like that
Can you believe, as you look at him
he's wearing a Chicago Bulls Basketball hat

2
There's a guy just been on TV
he's an all American superstar kid
he's a freedom fighter for his people
though it's making him a million quid
he says his people are starving
no food and things like that
Can you believe, as you look at him
he's wearing a Chicago Bulls Basketball hat

3
There's a guy just been on TV
from some South American despot's state
he's a drugs baron multi-millionaire
still wears a cap to hide his face
he keeps his people starving
no food and things like that
And you'd better believe me buddy
he's wearing a Chicago Bulls Basketball hat

4
I'm just a guy sat watching a video
the Live Aid video makes me feel so fat
thousands of homeless people starving
no food and things like that

Feed the World is a simplified answer
yet it crossed my mind as I sat,
that advertising pays, that's the philosophy
from a Chicago Bulls Basketball hat

****

Note
SITTING WATCHING TV ONE NIGHT STRUCK ME AS REALLY
WEIRD THAT AMONGST ALL THE POVERTY FIGHTING
BLOODSHED WAS SOME FREAK ADVERTISING
****

COLD EYES
© Gordon martin

1
One thing I can't stand,
is people with a supercilious look on their face
like they know something you don't
and then they just get on your case

2
What a negative attitude to have
what a shallow life they lead
when the night's prime entertainment
is conceived to watch you bleed

3
Just show me someone who doesn't
carry a scar of a mistake or regret
and I'll show you in that person
someone that hasn't even lived as yet

4
So take that look from your face
and think before you criticize
and know that I see what lies
behind the smile and those cold, cold eyes

****
Note:
I went to a party once, and someone there was really getting slagged off.
Now I had no special feelings for this person, but the thing that irritated me
most was this attitude of having something on someone.
Hence this.
****

Gordon on his appointment to
Head of Finance at Beezer c.1984

FOOTBALL? WHO WANTS FOOTBALL?
© Gordon martin

THE SET UP

Busy putting plans together
for Saturday's motorway meet.

The northern scum from Manchester
and the Arsenal elite.

OK lads we set it up
for Leicester Forest East

And you kick the shit and fight the scum
like you're a wild beast

The puny red shirt drongos
won't know the time or day

In fact they never would again boys
if I could have my way.

Stanley knives to cut them
cycle chains to maim and bruise

Petrol bombs to blow them up
come on lads, it's time to choose.

They'll get what's coming to them
we'll show them we're the boys

And send them snivelling home to ma and pa
and back to their cuddly toys

THE LAW

Police surveillance here, Chief Constable,
yes, we know that there's a meet.

We've infiltrated the organization
rest assured, our planning is discreet..

Rather control it at the services
in a limited space restricted site

No point in letting them run the streets
in an open warfare city fight

THE MEET

OK boys they're due here at high noon,
got here early, we're ready for their games

What the fuck was that explosion?
Shit, my car's just gone up in a mass of flames!

The scum are already here, boys,
look around they're everywhere,

Sod it, the Old Bill's here as well, boys,
I can see them over there!

The Manchester lads were at them,
the whole scene was like a war,
the police waded in with truncheons,
and soon levelled up the score.
In five minutes it was over,

police vans in rows, carting thugs away
and sanity prevailed for once,
and law and order won the day.

THE AFTERMATH

I have heard the evidence before me
You don't show me any remorse

Nor do you have respect for anyone
whether civilian or police force

You will go to jail for eighteen months.
Officer, take the prisoner down,

And he leant over to his colleague,
and hid his mouth with a sleeve of his gown.

If I had the power, he whispered,
I'd give them two years, or even three

or lock them up forever,
and throw away the key!

INNOCENCE LOST
© **Gordon martin**

1
Ghosts of ideals set aside,
withdrawn ambition and buried pride,
relentless the oncoming tide,
innocence nowhere to hide.

2
Uncoordinated are the steps I take
unrelenting the pain of deep heartache
unbelievable the route I make
undeniable the fool's mistake

3
Haunting visions blur my eyes
misty and confused surprise
where once I aimed for glittering prize
innocence lays wounded by mistaken lies

4
Doubting every word I say
discounting truth along the way
disenfranchised freedom the price to pay
deserving hurt I feel today

5
Experience is not always kind
it rides the helter skelter of your mind
until you are deaf and dumb and blind
and left wondering will you ever find
........innocence lost
?

IT'S A MYSTERY
©Gordon martin

EVERY SATURDAY NIGHT I WATCH HER

I THINK IT'S DEEPER THAN JUST LOVE

I PUT HER ON A PEDESTAL

AND THANK THE LORD ABOVE

BUT THOUGH I AM DEVOTED

SHE NEVER CALLS ME AND I'M BLUE

OH RISK IT, MEG

MY MYSTIC MEG

JUST SAY

GORDON WILL BE CELEBRATING TOOOOO!

****

Note:
Mystic Meg - advertising for the National Lottery
****

Kill The Beast
© Gordon martin

1
You can party all night
next day you don't feel right
you can diet and slim
to look just right for him
live life solely for fun
but it's Russian roulette with a gun
and enough is a feast
IT'S TIME TO KILL THE BEAST

2
I can go watch the game
shoot for fortune or fame
work like a horse
deal on the golf course
but it won't last forever
sooner or later not never
most likely not least
IF I DON'T KILL THE BEAST

3
So let's stay home tonight
Perhaps watch the fight
have some wine and a meal
How's that for a deal
make plans for some fun
somewhere quiet with sun
watch it rise in the east
WHEN WE'VE KILLED THE BEAST

4
and paid our respects to the deceased
WHEN WE'VE BURIED THE BEAST

Just A Kind Old Lady
© **Gordon martin**

1
The house was wrecked, from bottom to top,
seems that once they started, they couldn't stop.
They beat the owner black and blue,
a widowed old lady of eighty-two.

2
They left her bleeding, shaking, weeping,
a broken photo, she was keeping,
lay on the floor, beside her head,
on a freezing night, couldn't reach her bed
only inches from its warmth she lay,
praying that they'd go away.

3
And soon the kicking, jeering, swearing,
was over, and as she laid there, staring,
at the photograph, of her soldier son,
torn and ripped and spat upon,
she broke down, and gave one last deep sigh.
Is this a way, that a lady should die?

4
So all you people, who wish to do good,
and help the poor criminal be understood,
remember this old lady's plight,
and thank God it wasn't you on that night.
And to each one of you that murdered and stole
may the devil forever torment your soul!

****

Note
Help the victim, punish the guilty
****

LADY
© **Gordon martin**

Like morning's first light, after night's deep dark pile,

I'm washed in the warmth of your radiant smile.

The way that you care, and take time out for me,

will be cherished and remembered through eternity

You're there giving warmth on a cold stormy day

And if l want some good loving I just have to say

and people will always remember you for

the way you take time out to help when they come to your door

I'm so glad I wed you and gave you my name

pride will always burn in me like an eternal flame

You're my leading lady

You're my heart's one desire

You're the belle of the ball

Baby, come light my fire!

Gordon and Maureen, Wedding day 1986

THE DREAM
© Gordon martin 1994

1
It's the middle of winter
there a frost in the air
the roads are all frozen
No-one's going anywhere

2
Except me 'cause I'm stupid
well at least in this dream
I'm going to join
Britain's ski jumping team

3
And now I'm standing
At the top of the slope
too late to retreat
just do it and hope

4
I'm flying down faster
than a bat out of hell
I'm out of control
It's easy to tell

5
I'm throwing myself off
of the edge of the run
and hurtling through space
doing more than a ton

6
The ground's coming up
faster than I'm descending
will I get to land safely
what will be the ending

7
I crash in a pile
and I'm starting to weep
when I hear a voice saying
"Gordon, please go to sleep!"

Has The World Gone Mad?

© Gordon martin 1994

1
Has the world gone mad or am I thick
Addicts getting totally stoned, just for a kick
Stealing from innocent people is one of their tricks
Just so they can get another quick fix

2
Marching for a cause is admirable and fine
I wish someone would start a march for mine
But wanton destruction along the way?
I wouldn't give them the time of the day

3
When children are no longer able to walk
To the corner shop, and with people talk
Without fear of being stalked approached or seduced
Mishandled, mistreated, abducted, abused

4
When senior citizens stay home in fear
Because a friend was mugged for the price of a beer
Walking only a mile to pick up their pension
Does life have any meaning or comprehension

5
When the kid that's walking down the street
Thinks it's tough to knock you off your feet
Or shout verbal abuse, or stare at you
Because that's what he feels like he wants to do

6
If you have an opinion someone doesn't like
Why do they think they have the right
To get some mates to gather round
And beat you senseless into the ground

7
But after all what can you expect
How will they ever have any respect
When they're allowed to walk out free on bail
Instead of throwing them all in jail

8
Some social workers think they need attention
But that's something you stand to when you're in detention
Why should they live a life of luxury
When the victim is left to struggle emotionally

9
Until we allow the police to bite back
With the best form of defence; attack
To root out those who violate and rob
And give them the tools to do the job

10
Why should we even be concerned today
If a violent psychopath is blown away
It's time to react and start fighting for
The underdog, the invalid and the poor

11
Hit the criminals hard and heavy I say
Take their possessions if they try not to pay
Stop showing concern for the scum and dirt
And spare a thought for the people they hurt

12
I can't believe people show more fuss and concern
For some crazy or weirdo who refuses to learn
That you can't just do whatever you feel
Without taking other peoples' rights into the deal

13
Has the world gone mad or am I alone
In thinking I should be safe in my own home
And free to walk along a city street
And not be worried what kind of person I might meet

HAVE YOU GOT THE TIME?
© **Gordon martin 1994**

1
He dodged the splashing water
from the spray the car had made
as he looked across the road
just past the shopping arcade

2
It was hard to make out anything
in the heavy driving rain
and the lightning cracked and thunder roared
and he wished he was home again

3
But he couldn't miss the chance
to make contact with the girl
he'd tried for months to get to know
and his head began to swirl

4
He got to talk to her earlier
and asked her for a date
and if she'd got the time. She said,
"Yes, be at this address at eight"

5
So now its almost five to eight
and he approaches the designated plot
his heart starts beating faster
his stomach is in a knot

6
He arrives at the door at last
but much to his surprise
upon the sign beside the door
the following legend held his eyes

7
You enter because you want to
not through any force majeure
but when you step across the line
and behind you close the door

8
there'll be no going back
for what you do inside
has never been done by man before
so be sure before you decide

9
He hesitated for a while
somehow he knew it wasn't a prank
he opened the door and peered inside
and for a moment his spirit sank

10
In front a long narrow hallway
a grey wall to either side
no internal lights to illuminate
what the dark far side door might hide

11
He took a deep breath and stepped inside
thinking what have I got to lose
there's really only one option
that a curious man could choose

12
He quickly made his way over
to the darkened door that he had seen
and heard the entrance door creak shut
like in a horror movie scene

13
He knocked upon the door
in a positive sort of way
and when there was no answer
decided to go in anyway

14
The room was just like many
you might enter every day
clean, tidy and presentable
nothing unusual you might say

15
Then across the far side of the room
someone opened another door
and there in front of him now stood
the girl that he met before

16
"You asked me for the time" she said
"and also for a date,
you now must choose the same yourself,
as the offer I reciprocate"

17
"What is this?" he asked nervously
"some weird kind of game.
What are you on, some kind of fix,
or are you just insane?"

18
"Oh no," she replied "it's as I said,
of that there is no doubt,
you read the sign but still came in.
too late for wanting out

19
Now make your choice, you can't escape
Nor do me any ill
the first date and time you utter
is yours to command at will

20
You will instantly go to that date and time
that you select, I give my word
but where on earth you appear
will be the place the most important thing occurred

21
So make your decision carefully
and use this solitary choice
You will have the power to change history
and in that the whole world may rejoice"

22
"I'll go along with this," he said
"and put my name on the line"
He gave the girl a time of day
And chose 1889

23
And suddenly he transposed
from that room to another
where he's speaking a foreign language
to someone about to become a mother

24
And the husband is there beside him
he's a customs officer somewhere
He's saying to our time traveller
"Doctor please take care"

25
And just as before it's raining
thunder and lightning too
the day is as black as a witch's cat
the child is born, a life anew

26
He holds the baby in his hands
It's helpless, he has the power to destroy
"I think we'll call him Adolf," says Herr Hitler
"It's a nice name for a boy"

WOMAN

1

The girl holds her mother's hand
she's going to meet her friends
it's a birthday treat her mother planned
she hopes it never ends
she's five today and all her pals
will be giving her a present
they gather round and make a fuss
it's starting to look so pleasant

2

The old lady of ninety five breathes deep
and fills her lungs with air
the pain she feels inside her chest
is getting hard to bear
she's weary of being in hospital
will they ever make her fit
right now she'd feel successful
if she managed to rise and sit

3

The young girl is on a buzz
she's off to meet her mate
they're going dancing to the nightclub
they know they'll be out late
they've got two Friday night specials
meeting them at ten or so
then it's action through to two or three
have fun, go with the flow

4

Today's the day that she's retiring
and so she finishes work for good
looking back it seemed just yesterday
at the factory gates she stood

wondering what it would be like
having to work to earn a living,
school gone forever, never to return
but for that she'd no misgiving

5
A mother of two, one girl, one boy
and not yet twenty five
married to a drunken animal
stuck inside this two room dive
she's got to get away from this
it's twisting like a knife
no longer a happy carefree girl
but a suppressed despondent wife

6
Her fortieth birthday comes around,
the girls are planning to hit the town.
(she's divorced, her children nearly grown)
and they'll be letting their hair down.
Start off drinking around the pubs
onto the dance club, do the hustle
have a laugh enjoy themselves,
and maybe pull a bit of muscle.

7
Seventy five, she feels alive
no problems, she's quite fit
married twice, this one is nice
even though he's getting on a bit.
You couldn't ever want a man
to be different in any way
they're so happy with each other
and look forward to each new day

8
I finally managed to rid myself
of that stupid ugly jerk

now I can get my life together
start rebuilding get some work.
At least the weight is off my shoulders
and I really feel good
I never thought I'd feel this way again
though my friends all said I would

9
Mum died so suddenly yesterday
I don't think that I can cope
My past in realisation,
present shoulder, future hope.
She was everything and more to me
She was comparable with no other
She was the very essence of the word
in every way a perfect mother

10
I'll always remember the summer night
we sat on the beach in Spain
how he gently held me close to him
and how we ran in from the rain.
But we still got soaking wet
and so we took a shower together
we knew each other for such a short time
but he's in my heart forever.

11
Good men, bad men, kind men, rough,
considerate, selfish, timid, tough,
young boys at forty, men at eighteen,
I've lived a life, a lot I've seen,
and so when my time is over
it won't be a life of regret
and don't think you're rid of me so soon
I'm not planning on going yet

12
In the hospital ward, a baby girl is born
to the delight of her proud mother
and above the story of her life
as normal as any other,
Mixed up, but that's how life itself
seems to be from time to time
an innocent life is put on earth
it's good we can't see the hills to climb

13
You take the rough, you take the smooth
you take whatever life puts before you
and make of it the best you can
no words were ever said more true.

Parents in Law Eddie and Jenny 1986

Gordon and Maureen on holiday c.1987

Remember

Remember walking through the alleys
And over the canals in Venice
And the day we climbed the Eiffel tower
Or sat by Notre Dame in Paris
When I was stunned
By Niagara Falls' power on first sight
The glitz and the glamour of Vegas at night
The Pyramids and Sphinx were fascinating to see
And remember standing in Sorrento
And looking out to Capri
Walking the chariot rutted streets of Pompeii nearby
Just imagining Vesuvius erupting, hot ash in the sky
Spending one day in New York's skyscraper metropolis
And the next in Huntsville where everything seemed motionless
How we stood at the spot where Jesus was born
And saw Gethsemane,
The memories go on and on
The times that we've stood on Spain's golden sands
The tranquillity we felt when we walked home holding hands
In St. Pete's Beach in the evening, and to return was our pledge
How we amazed at the Grand Canyon as we flew over the edge
The fun we had in Toronto that Fall
I remember it well,
I remember it all
But the thing that gave these journeys a magical hue
Was simply the fact that
I went there with you

THE MEN IN WHITE COATS

1
The men in white coats arrived the other day
They act like they think they're God
But when they arrived I'd already gone
Big Ears had given me the nod

2
He told me they'd be coming
When we sat with Snowy and Tin Tin
At the entrance to the Pleasure Dome
And we watched the crowd come in

3
So I only had time to stop and watch
The first two acts overall
On first was the Klinsmann School of Tumbling
And boy does he know how to fall

4
The other was a group of clowns
Who just kept getting in each others way
I've since heard they've left the circus
And are running the country today

5
But me, I'm still on the run
They haven't caught me yet
They missed me at Lord Lucan's reunion bash
Just how lucky can you get

6
As it finished the doors burst open
and in ran a man holding a straightjacket
But he mistook me for Donald Trump
And asked me how he could make a packet

7
I fell about in hysterical fits
I couldn't believe this was happening
In fact if it wasn't so funny
You could almost find it frightening

8
The only conclusion I could draw
From being considered Donald Trump's double
Was that things were getting worse by the minute
and I was in a load more trouble

9
Meanwhile the man from the Institute
Was dragging Trump down into the cellar
And people were asking me for money
I told them to contact Rockefeller

10
I slipped out through the backdoor
It's a trick I often used
If I was getting harangued by men in white
Or my pride was getting bruised

11
I ran down the road as fast as Linford could
My feet hardly touched the ground
I didn't even stop to talk to Lord Canaervon
About the ancient tombs he said he'd found

12
And I was glad about it later
When someone told me about the curse
When you're in a load of trouble
You know there's nothing worse

13
The last thing that I wanted that night
As I slept content in bed
Was a visit from Tutankhamen,
His mummy and the living dead

14
But you know I had the strangest dream
We were all in the reincarnation room
Drawing lots to see who got to be a success
And who was destined for a life of doom

15
There were six of us in our group
Three short straws and three more long
I was the last but one to draw a straw
And two of each had gone

16
I took a deep breath and studied hard
I had to go for broke
Heaven or hell for seventy years
And guess what, that's when I awoke

17
The knocking on the door made me jump
And I looked around the curtain
The men in white were back I think
But in the dark I wasn't certain

18
I decided to climb out of the window
And drop to the ground and split
But in the heat of the moment forgot
I wasn't wearing any kit

19
And wouldn't you know when you don't want one
A policeman always appears
He arrested me and threw me in jail
And said I was looking at twenty years

20
Twenty years for standing outside my house
Minding my own business in the dark
You could say that I was angry
With this blue uniformed bright spark

21
But I needed to get of there
My pursuers saw him throw me in the car
I said will 50 quid be enough
And remember me to your ma

22
And here's another fifty
For the shirt and trousers. I suppose
That now I've got you thinking
How I had money but no clothes

23
OK I'll tell you how I did it
I've a hundred in my socks, it's true
And any self respecting cowboy
Always sleeps with *his* boots on too

24
The cop was more than helpful
He quickly swallowed up his pride
And muttered don't come round here no more
And leave the money on the side

25
Out of the front door of the gaol
Looking forward to be free
When all at once twelve heavy men
Came from nowhere and jumped on me

26
This time there was no escape
You can't win all the time
And anyway I've got to find a way
To finish off this rhyme

27
So now I spend my days
In a padded cell ad infinitum
But I have a lot of fun
The lunatics have taken over the asylum

Keep Taking The Tablets
©Gordon martin 1994

1
I was feeling confused and weary
So I went to my GP
He said sit down, took out a hammer
And hit me on the knee
Your reflexes seem OK
Though your pulse is a little weak
He wrote out a prescription
And said come back in a week

2
So I popped across to the chemist
Who quickly dispensed the pills
And wrote on the label one a day
Will cure all of your ills
I said thanks a lot and hurried home
I made a cup of tea
And thought of taking two of them
But finally settled on taking three

3
It started with a tingle in my feet
And continued past my thighs
By the time it reached my waistline
I was buzzing to my surprise
And I was already regretting my foolishness
When my shoulders started to jump
And my face became distorted
And my head began to thump

4
My whole body was electric
I had to get outside
I ran straight through a window
And in fright, the cat nearly died

I shot across the road
Running as fast as Billy Whizz
As I overtook the marathon leader
He said "get me on some of his"

5

I ran alongside the railway line
And waved to the train driver as I passed
In forty-five minutes I hit London
And I was still travelling very fast
Down from London to the Channel tunnel
No sign of any deceleration
And in what seemed like only minutes
Was being welcomed by the French nation

6

I can't stop now, I'm in a rush
I shouted as I went through
The only words I caught in return
Were Bon Voyage and Sacre Bleu
Across the Alps like Hannibal
Down to Italy and into Milan
I stuck one in from Gullitt pass
While they were marking another man

7

I quickly did a U-turn
When I saw the Mediterranean sea
Anyway swimming to Libya and Gaddafi
Didn't seem like a good idea to me
And suddenly the third tablet
Is having an effect
I'm taking off just like an F-16
But this one's got no eject

8
So I put my fist out in front of me
Well that's what Superman would do
And I bank 20 degrees and hold my course
Until my house is back in view
Suddenly the effect of the tablets
Is beginning to subside
And I crash through the roof of my house
And this time the cat has died

9
The moral of this story is to
Follow instructions and that is that
Oh except for one other point
Avoid keeping a nervous cat

Maureen, Andrew, David and Gordon
August 1987, just weeks after his diagnosis with Parkinsons

Fame At Last

© Gordon martin 1994**© Gordon martin 1994**

1
So you finally hit the big time
You'll be seen and talked about
When you put your Italian suit on
And take one of your girlfriends out

2
And when fame comes along
You'll grasp and hold it with both hands
And pick who you want to talk to
And who will carry out your demands

3
Expect people to treat you like a king
And bow as you walk past
And speak only if you speak to them
Your reputation is spreading fast

4
You've got yourself a fast car
And gold around your neck
If you want some new possession
You just write another cheque

5
But forgive me if I'm not impressed
Or cow-tow when you're in view
Don't forget that I'm the one
Who was there when no-one wanted you

6
And I'll always be the person
Who stood with you against the tide
And protected you from criticism
And stood man to man at your side

7

So go and enjoy your days of success
And your cornucopia of plenty
But don't ever forget I knew you
Before you met the Cognoscenti

For Ivy
© Gordon martin 1994

1
Australia, I came to live with you
When my parents started a life anew
And l was just a girl some ten years old
And the future before me as yet to unfold

2
Now many years have passed me by
Changes I've seen made me laugh, made me cry
And I'm back in England with a family long parted
In the land of my birth, where my life story started

3
How different are these two worlds I travel between
An antipodal transformation everywhere to be seen
No kangaroos, no wombats, no rosella, no possum,
No koalas in eucalyptus trees as they blossom

4
But history abounds in the places passed through
York's city walls and Shambles and the Minster too
All the Norman churches and the castles out there
Westminster Abbey, St. Paul's and Trafalgar Square

5
It's been an emotional reunion, an experience too fast
Going back in my mind and reliving the past
And as I consider this land was my root
I come to realise the truth absolute

6
Australia is home and ever will be
While there's one drop of water left in the Tasman sea
And no irresistible object or immovable force
Could stop me from returning to my journey's source

7
Back to the land where my home and heart lie
To the vast open spaces under Australian sky
Over many a nation, ocean and sea
To the one who is waiting there quietly for me

WAITING FOR MY BABY
©Gordon martin 1994

1
Waiting for the kettle
Waiting for the post
Waiting for my baby
That's what I want the most

2
Waiting while I eat some toast
Waiting while l walk the path
Waiting while l drink some coffee
Waiting while l take a bath

3
Waiting in the heat of day
Waiting when the night turns cool
Waiting in the armchair
Waiting on the stool

4
Waiting in the kitchen
Waiting in the car
Waiting as the sun goes down
Waiting as I see a shooting star

5
Waiting counting seconds
Waiting while they tick away
Waiting for my baby
She's been out of town all day

6
Waiting for the telephone call
We're just getting on the train
Can you pick me up from the station
I'd like to go again

7
Waiting on the platform
I've got such a lot to say
We got a lot of bargains
Did you have a pleasant day

8
Waiting was it worth it
Wait a minute can't you see
Baby's had a fun day out
But she's glad she's back with me

9
And I'm happy that she's happy
And she knows I love her so
Makes the waiting all worthwhile
Each time I see her go

10
Absence makes the heart grow fonder
According to the proverb old
Waiting for my baby is proof positive
No line was ever better told

Gordon at Meadowlands, New York
Giants football stadium 1989

How Come?
© Gordon martin 1994

1
You're spending all your time at the local video dome
watching films of Arnold Schwarzenegger and Sylvester Stallone
So how come when there's trouble.
I'm left standing on my own.

2
You listen to the rock stars saying "take note of this, cool dude,
you should rebel against authority, discipline and attitude"
So how come when you're hungry
You come to me for food

3
You want to be independent, and put on your own show
Without any hassle from the people that you know
How come when you're left to it
You've got nowhere else to go

4
Don't think I'm trying to get involved
in matters that don't concern
It's just you're getting bad advice
and one day you'll have to learn

5
That tough guys rarely make a scene
Or have buzz words at the ready
And rock stars who rave on stage
are otherwise quite steady

6
They're making lots of cash
From singing songs that excite you
And if you want some independence
Here's what you ought to do

7
Get yourself a partner
Or perhaps a mate or two
Get a flat, share the cost
Stop being negative and blue

8
Start taking life for what it is
Enjoy each bright new day
Be cheerful and be happy
As you tread life's long highway

9
If you don't I'll tell you now
and from me the message is free
with three score years and ten to do
life's too long a misery

SUMMER'S PASSED
© **Gordon martin 1994**

1
Summertime draws to a close
There's a chill in the evening air
Anyone with any sense at all
Is going on holiday somewhere

2
The laziness of a hot summer day
Is dissolving in the autumn rain
Did we really want the heat to subside
As we rush for cover again

3
And the clouds roll by
and the leaves fall down
as the night draws in
on a northern town

4
Sitting on the platform
Waiting for the train
With a thousand people
All without a name

5
All these people that stand about me
Are like strangers from a foreign shore
Where once I identified with them
They don't connect with me anymore

6
What exactly am I doing here
How many times have you asked yourself that
Is it just the mood you're in today
Or something deeper than that

7
And a tramp walks by
and the leaves fall down
and the nights draw in
on a northern town

8
Sitting on the platform
Waiting for the train
Carry me back to my lady
Before I go insane

9
And massive white wisps of ice crystals
now fill the sky with snow
The sort that when you're driving
mesmerise you with relentless flow

10
And the hunger builds inside you
To be home in the warmth and calm
Of the world you built for relaxation
Free from craziness and harm

11
And the clock ticks by
and the leaves fall down
and the nights draw in
on a northern town

12
Sitting on the platform
Waiting for the train
It's entering the station
Soon I'll be home again

13
Opening the door at last
into the place that's best
Get down in the easy chair
Take a well earned rest

14
Lady and I sit talking
Until we realize the time that has elapsed
And head off to the bedroom
And forget that summer's passed.

THE ALCOHOLIC'S LAMENT
© Gordon martin 1994

1
I can hear the television from the room below
The newsman's telling yet another tale of misery and woe
And you know I could be out of here
If I had somewhere to go

2
I started taking whiskey but I soon became immune
They moved me from the clinic said there wasn't any room
So now to get a bed at night
I'm down to pushing broom

3
As I lay here broke but sober, a common state for me
That happens every time the days in a week add up to more than
three
The voice downstairs announces
Another tragedy at sea

4
The voice goes round and round, and round again inside my head
The continual drone. Another bad news day, its all that's ever read
Another third world revolution
Another thousand people dead

5
I'd like to say to the man below, switch that bloody television off
But he's the guy that runs this five dollar dive, and you're out if you
even cough
His manners are reminiscent
Of a pig eating from a trough

6
Do I have to lay here listening to this, outside it's pouring with rain
The choice, no choice at all but Hobson's, is pneumonia or go insane
So I guess I'm out of here for good
And I'm on the road again

7
I'm walking down the highway, that's so awash it's more like sea
This driving rain beating in my face will be the death of me
But I'm feeling optimistic
I'm only two days from a fee

8
And then for a short while I can once again turn into my alter ego
Consciousness to oblivion and back again, a three day to and fro
And so it turns around again
It's the only world I know.

THE CASE OF THE KILLER UMBRELLA

© Gordon martin 1994

1
You've heard many stories of outlaws
Like Billy the Kid and Ned Kelly, the bushranger
But the story you're about to read
Is as true but very much stranger

2
It's the story of an unassuming man
In fact quite an amiable fella
Who left London a trail of destruction
In The Case Of The Killer Umbrella

3
The story is recited
First hand by that very man
So listen to it carefully
And picture if you can..,,,,.,,,..

4
I was proceeding down the high street
Doing nobody any harm
When my arm began to jump and twitch
From previously being calm

5
I was carrying a carrier
(that seems a logical thing to do)
Inside were sports cards purchased
Approximately a thousand and two

6
Also in the bag was a purchase
Made earlier in the day
An automatic umbrella bought
To keep the rain out of the way

133

7
As I held the handle
I felt the button on the stock
And with a twitch of the arm pressed it
Was I in for a shock

8
The umbrella exploded open
It's an accurate word to use
The carrier torn to pieces
But here's the distressing news

9
An old lady out to walk the dog
Happened at that moment to pass by
And the umbrella crucified the dog
As it hit it in the eye

10
The old lady was mortified
In fact she turned to stone
I was praying for forgiveness
And hoping she was alone

11
Where were you Mo and Ivy
When I needed a little aid
Cards were flying everywhere
It looked like a German air raid

12
I casually glanced around
With an innocent smile and air
Hoping no-one really noticed
I counted fifty with a stare

13
Another fifty with outrage and anger
There was trouble, and I was in it
The only way out of this
Was to collect my cards and split

14
But I needed another bag
To put my belongings in
And having extracted the umbrella
Saw a CD shop and went in

15
I said I'll buy this CD
And offered cash to the man
And when you find a carrier for it
Give me the biggest that you can

16
He said ok and offered me
A very very large bag
But with umbrella and dog eye, cards and cash
My spirit was beginning to sag

17
How many hands do you think I've got
I asked with no reply
I think that he was transfixed
By the dog's cold staring eye

18
I managed to get it all together
And headed for the door
And back across to North London
Where Mo and Ivy were for sure

19
When they saw me coming
They said have you enjoyed the afternoon
I thought shall I tell them now
Or is it still too soon

20
Fearing half the police in London
Would now be on my trail
I said let's blow this town away
And so for home we soon set sail

21
The story was recounted
As I drove up the M1 fast
All I got was an hour of laughter
I was just glad the episode had passed

22
So now I think sometimes
Of going to the city
But the police, the woman and a host of others
Stop me going, what a pity!

You'll Never Be Famous (Gail's Poem)

© Gordon martin 1994

1

What can I say it's too late now
You called the future right
You'll never be famous
Just children's words
Said seriously one distant night

2

Well I guess we never reached the top
But girl we had fun trying
So, we missed out on fame
Who cares we lived
You won't hear me sat sighing

3

We went our ways both separately
But were always near at hand
Looking over one shoulder
At each other
And how our lives were planned

4

And we've never really been apart
Not in the truest sense
Nor have we left behind
The Brother
The feeling's still intense

5

And I guess for once I'll cut the jokes
And be honest when I say
That you're such
A special person to me
A perfect sister in every way

Gordon at Niagara Falls, 1989

Forget The Seals

© Gordon martin 1994

1
They say the seal population is in excess
If we don't control it we'll be in a mess
Well, I look at the world and see misery and pain
From country to country, over and over again

2
Perhaps we ought to consider human nature first
And care for the people whose lives have been cursed
By dictators with power through bullet and gun
To be the last ones to suffer the first ones to run

3
I say let's leave the seals to play in the sea
I've a better idea that's occurring to me
Take a look at the world and its pitiful face
Forget the seals, cull the human race

4
Start with the warmongers, then take trash
That murder innocent people in their search for cash
Next take the drug dealers who make misery for masses
And perhaps then we'll see that a new dawn passes

5
And then people could start to live a life free
From oppression and duress, what a world that would be
People going about their life happy, content
And the seals swim the seas as God surely meant

PARKINSONISM FOR THE LAYMAN
© Gordon martin 1994

1
Parkinsonism for the layman
How's that for an eye catching leader
To producing a one page rhyming guide
Explaining medical terms that baffle the reader

2
Paralysis Agitans is Parkinsonism
To give it a medical name
Both words name the condition
And mean exactly the same

3
Tremor is another word for shaking
Rigidity is when your muscles freeze
Akinesia the inability to start to move
Or perform actions naturally or with ease

4
When you have this problem
You could be described as akinetic
And defective blood supply to the basal ganglia
Would best describe Arteriosclerotic

5
Produced by the brain to help the passage
Of information through the nervous system there
Is a chemical substance called Dopamine
In Parkinsonism a shortfall will occur

6
L dopa or Levadopa is the chemical name for the drug
Used to increase the level of Dopamine
Which will hopefully - and usually - result in
An improvement in the condition being seen

7
Dyskenesia is the medical term
For the involuntary movement that's produced
By too high a dose of Levadopa
And can be alleviated if the intake is reduced

8
Basal Ganglia and Nuclei are names
For part of the extra pyramidal system
Which is simply where the Dopamine shortage occurs
In the brain and nervous System

9
Monotonous speech is a symptom
This is talking in one tone
Very similar to listening to a broadcast
Of a politician's constant boring drone

10
These lines are merely a quick guide
To help you understand and not resist
The medical terminology, but is not intended,
Nor could be, a substitute for talking to a specialist.

Earth Calling.....Earth Calling........ Are You Receiving?

© Gordon martin 1994

1
I must say that this whole thing is now well out of hand
You couldn't have made a bigger mess if you had it planned
You must be the biggest idiot
The length and breadth of the land

2
Why don't you get off the cloud you're living on
And come back down to earth
Stop talking telephone numbers
Who cares how much you're worth

3
I can't believe that I'm still hearing the same tune after all these years
And that the women that you're connecting with are all misery and tears
You should show some consideration
And allay some of their fears

4
Why don't you get off the cloud you're living on
And come back down to land
Declare your intentions truthfully
State what you've really got planned

5
How many times must you have to be asked
Before we get to know
Are you coming or going, or are you just standing still
Is there any intent, or is it all an elaborate show

6

Why don't you get off the cloud you're living on
And come back down where the air is less thin
Lets see some action not words, you're living not dead
Or has rigor mortis already set in

7

Just get off your backside and do something once and for all
Make a decision, stop wondering if you'll stand or you'll fall
Go the way that you want to,
But please make the call

8

And when you've got off the cloud that you're living on
And come down and shown that you can relate
Instead of walking around with your head in the clouds
You might find that it's not yet too late

Is That The Express Train Coming?

© Gordon martin 1994

1

Another day has started
I'm sitting in my chair
I've taken my first dose of drugs
My face just wears a stare
My body aches in all my joints
My limbs are rigid and dead
As I sit here waiting for release
A thousand thoughts go through my head

2

How long can I put up with this
Forty four and no sign of a cure
A life that's on hold for thirty plus years?
That's a long time to endure
And I know that it's not stable
That the slope that I'm standing upon
Is forever turning downwards
And gets darker as I trudge on

3

As I laid in bed this morning
With my lady by my side
I knew that I couldn't move to her
And that really knocks your pride
And she tries to be kind and patient
And tells me it's alright
But I just want to be as I was
And forget another long dark night

4

And so I move in shuffles
Across the floor to my computer chair
And in putting feelings into print
Find some mental release there

A hope these words might soon be read
In some magazine or book
And some rich philanthropist is moved to action
When by chance he takes a look

5
"There must be some way out of here
Said the joker to the thief,"
Words written by Dylan long ago
Keep me hoping for release
Parkinsonism is both these things -
A joker and a thief
Switching mobility for paralysis and back again
Taking self respect for grief

6
"There's too much confusion"
Dylan then goes on to say
Words that I can identify with
As I sit here shaking today
I know that progress is being made
And with that faint hope I endure
In the words of the aforesaid poet
"There's a slow train coming" - but does it bring a cure?

7
If it does, then even though wishes are
For children and fools to cling to
Take it off the slow train, load it on the express
We'll all be there when it comes roaring through
And the cure will spread among us
And we'll bless the ones who found it
And thank the ones who brought it
And praise the ones that made it

8
And we'll stand together smiling
Free from this dreaded curse
And move freely to one another
And easily converse
And we'll all get release from this terrible shake
And at last find peace and calm
And my lady and I will slip away
And lay together arm in arm

For George
© **Gordon martin**

1
I sit in my lounge
and look across at the chair,
when my friend came to visit
would always sit there,
and I can see him there now,
with a brandy in hand,
as we talked of people and places,
things done and things planned.

2
I think of the day
he arranged especially for me,
and drove for four hours
just so I could see
The Williams Baseball Museum
at Citrus Hill Springs
and watched the pleasure I got
from souvenirs and such things.

3
Everything had gone wrong
with his car on that day.
The radiator and tyre
had both given way,
but he never relented,
the museum his sole view,
and he'd get there, whatever,
so determined to get through.

4

It wasn't so long, either,
that a recovery he'd made,
after an operation in hospital,
and was in a bed laid.
That day confirmed my belief,
though I knew long before,
what a good friend he was:
honest, helpful and sure.

5

So now as I sit
and picture him there,
and tears fill my eyes,
and my heart's in despair,
I think of our vow, said
as we returned home, later, that night,
That we'd be friends forever.
Well, George, you were right.

Gordon in Paris for his 40th Birthday, 1990

I Don't Understand
© Gordon martin

1
When I was a lad
Of just fourteen years
My brother passed away
It reduced me to tears

2
And over the years
Others close have departed
Family for life
Friendship just started

3
Caring loving people
Like Eddie and Jen
I form a close bond
And it happens again

4
As the new year dawned
And the old came to an end
Once more sweet Jesus
You took my best friend

5
And if I live for eternity
Or search the entire land
The reason why it is so
I'll never understand

6
Why people not worth giving
The time of the day
Live on for ever and ever
And good men are taken away.

A RIGHT CHARLIE
© **Gordon martin**

1
Charlie please tell me
What do you want out of life
You have lots of money
You had a good wife

2
Don't you think that
The masses feel pain just like you
They don't have your money
And their blood isn't blue

3
Do you want invisibility
Do you want to be free
Do you want leaving alone
An ordinary guy just like me

4
Well Charlie you know
You really shouldn't complain
That you were born in high office
That you have the best name

5
There's many a man
I meet everyday
Who would gladly swap places
And swap straightaway

6
Good men who have toiled
For years and what for
Some food on the table
And carpets on floor

7
And many a good woman
Looked after her man well
Do you think that you've found one
Do you think you could tell

8
People carry on daily
Too proud to complain
But when I read a newspaper
It's about you again

9
Charlie please tell me
You'll make up your mind
And stop fussing and fighting
And act more like my kind

FRIENDSHIP
© Gordon martin

1
This poem is for friendship for people who care
The ones who'd come running if you wanted them there.

2
The people who stand by your side in distress
The people who'd help you get out of a mess

3
The people who don't ask a reason you call
They just rally and help when you stumble and fall

4
The people who believe in fair play and are true
They stand their own corner not lean upon you

5
And I take this opportunity to name names : here I go
Thanks Martin, thanks Diana, thanks Kev and thanks Geo.

6
Although only recently have I known you all well
I'm glad you're my friends but I guess you can tell

7
When all's said and done it's not the words I impart
It's what you see in the eyes and feel in the heart

The Phoney Preacher
© Gordon martin

1

His fist smashes on the table
His other hand raised high in the air
He waves it at the crowd convened
A bible held high there

2

"Listen to me sinners
Repent your evil ways
Bow your heads in homage
And with me, the good Lord Praise"

3

"Hallelujah" shouts a person
From amongst the gathered throng
"Praise the Lord", the man intercedes
"Forgive them for doing wrong"

4

"If you believe in Christ Almighty
And you want forgiveness for your sin
Walk to the front, and pray with me
With Jesus you will win

5

Come and sign to help this mission
Spread the word of the God throughout the nation
You'll walk with God, Bless you all
Please make a large donation"

6

The convention closes, the crowd head for home
The phoney preacher thinks he's scored
And now back at the motel room
He's beginning to get bored

7
"How much did we take today?"
He says to the man sat counting cash aloud
He's the same man that shouted "Hallelujah"
And stood up in the crowd

8
The first to walk to the front
To be forgiven for his sin
"We made two grand at least today,
Let's get a few good time girls to come in"

9
"And tonight we'll party , down some beer
Have fun then take a rest,
And tomorrow make our way down south
Where the pickings are the best"

10
"It sure beats working for a living"
the man still counting the cash says
"Just telling them to walk hand in hand with God
And mend their wicked ways"

11
The evangelist is laughing
But his smile turns to a frown
When the motel door bursts open
And a voice shouts out "Get down!"

12
"Get your hands behind your back.
Do it now!" the sheriff's loud voice booms.
He cuffs them both, then says to his man
"Deputy check these rooms."

13
Next he tells the evangelist, " You're bust
For robbery with violence,
At the book store twenty four hours ago.
You have a right to silence."

14
"Evangelism don't make me laugh
You never set foot in church
I can't believe you had the nerve
But now you're in the lurch"

15
"You had me fooled a while I guess
Until your confidence grew
And you asked me to attend the show
I suppose you're wondering how I knew"

16
"This morning when you asked the stooge
To pass the bible over there
He gave you one he took from the store
And when you waved it in the air

17
I recognised it, and the store man's words
Recalled from the day before
There were only five specially made
And he's still got the other four"

18
The morals of this story are that
Religion comes from within
And stealing cheating and lying
Are all defined as sin

19
So don't play at being holy
And don't trick your fellow man
For as sure as there's a Good Lord above
You'll end up in the can

20
And if by chance you don't
And live life free to your last dying bone
Remember that there's a heaven and hell
And the Devil will take his own

****

The following limerick is based on true story which appeared in the Daily Mail 19.01.95

****

COCONUT SHY
© Gordon martin 1995

1
A Malaysian coconut grower named Mat Hussin
Spent a lot of time worrying and fussing
He trained a monkey you see to climb up a tree
To save him from huffing and puffing

2
There's a sad end to the tale I've just read
The monkey must have been poorly bred
Instead of hitting the deck he hit Mat on the neck
Who with the toss of a coconut was dead

3
Now Mat's gone to farm in the sky
With the angels and Jesus on high
He told God he'd farm beet or anything else you could eat
But remained eternally coconut shy!

ERIC CANTONA
A MESSAGE TO THE FOOTBALL ASSOCIATION
© Gordon martin

1
When the man has got the ball
He's a delight to watch - a dream
He's probably one of the finest players
The world has ever seen

2
But when a defender gets beaten by the skill
Of, a maestro the sport cries out for
He nudges trips or holds him
The only way to stop him score

3
How often must a man get kicked
How often must he wait
To get protection from amateur officials
Every time a tackle comes late

4
We never read in headlines
Of the players who give the stick
But when he retaliates it's shock horror
It really makes me sick

5
Don't tell me Eric goes out to kick
With skill he's away and gone
But you know that plodding defenders
Have it in their heads when they go on

6
The truth of the sending off at Arsenal
Is that he didn't even connect
Ask Tony Adams - he was the 'victim'
He'll tell you that's correct

7
At Galatasaray the whole match in truth
Was nothing but a joke
Eleven cynical Turks with one intent
To incite, inflame and provoke

8
At Crystal Palace the famous 'kick'
Was hardly powder puff
And this in a sport where defenders
Are super fit and tough

9
So that's three sending's off the game got wrong
Over half the total count
So when you judge his record
Just take that into account

10
And think in truth how you would feel
With a crowd hurling abuse at you
Don't tell me when you sit at home
You don't criticize them too

11
And the guy who remonstrates at a man
And is surprised when he fights back
And has the nerve to make a complaint
It really gets up my back

12
This is a guy who'd go in a pub
And tell his mates I really gave him what for
Just consider which side of football is wrong
When Eric's called to your door

13
If you walked down the street and got aggression
In a similar sort of way
You'd stand your ground, man to man
Not take it and slink away

14
The cops were there in numbers
Queuing up to take an 'unbiased' word
From a host of Crystal Palace fans
The whole thing really is absurd

15
Where were the same heroes in uniform
And where the stewards too
When the crowd were abusing Cantona
With language turning the cold night air blue

16
And where the consistency in refereeing
A tackle later in the game
On Ryan Giggs was ten times worse than that
But the referee only took his Name

17
So hound Eric, drive him from the game
And you'll find a new dawn pass
The standard of football will decline
The truth is you can't stand class.

Gordon with friends Nina and George in Las Vegas 1992

What Is Parkinsonism Like?

© Gordon martin

1
The most common thing that I am asked to explain
Is what exactly is Parkinsonism, is it some sort of pain?

2
Pain isn't the problem at least not at first
It's the inability to move freely that affects you the worst

3
One moment you're moving with consummate bliss
And then the condition takes over and you feel just like this:

4
Like being frozen stiff without any cold
Like someone has just put your whole life on hold

5
Like locked in a room without any key
But the room is my body and it's imprisoning me

6
Like just going out takes a real master plan
Like shopping for food whenever you can

7
Like smiling at someone but they see a stare
Like struggling to rise and get out of a chair

8
Like a nervous child who can't stop shaking
Like a man who has toiled and his body is aching

9
Like taking one step is an amazing success
Like thinking clearly but writing a mess

10
Like shaking your head for no reason at all
Like getting from A to B without having a fall

11
Like having people look at you and think
Is he so overpowered by an excess of drink

12
Like wanting someone to aid help and care
Then becoming confused and you wish they weren't there

13
Like standing transfixed like a man turned to stone
by the sight of the Gorgon and you feel so alone

14
Like putting clothes on becomes a major task
like needing help but being too proud to ask

15
Like trying to swallow but your throat is so dry
like wasting your life as another week passes by

16
Like wanting to travel but you know you won't go
like the on-off eternity is the one world you know

17
So how can I best describe this malaise
I've already done so in so many ways

18
But if I was asked just four lines to choose
the description below is the one I would use:

19
Like being in prison
Without any bars
Like being tortured
Without any scars

SEAGULLS
© Gordon martin

People get jealous when you have success
They'll try many tricks to make you a mess
Insults lies and defamation I guess
Anything to put you under more stress
The French have a saying
That aptly reflects this tragedy
When the seagulls follow the trawler
It's because they expect sardines
To be thrown into the sea

Ten Thousand Million Light Years
© Gordon martin

If life exists at the outer limits
of the boundary of the known universe
it would take ten thousand million light years
to reach there to converse
and in all that vast star covered wilderness
no other life form has ever been defined
so what is it that gave us blood in our veins
air to breath, and hearts, and minds
Can we accept the theory of Darwin
an ecological evolution
or is there something more besides
that can lead us to a solution
can Einstein solve the mystery
of how life on earth began
what changed us from wild animals
into logical thinking man
Do his theories on relativity
hold the key to explain the soul
will it unlock the door of concept
and make life's battered mosaic whole
and what of the pages of history
that amassed stories of religious crusade
can the teachings of men
whose belief is devout
be the place where the answer is laid
All I ask of you reader is to consider
the vastness of creating such
a grand master plan
Do you think mere mortals can form an opinion
without becoming egotistic pious and partisan
I suggest from a standpoint of blindness
and overwhelming ignorance of such an idea
The magnificence of God and His creation
could not be understood in those ten thousand million light years

DEJA-VU
© Gordon martin

1
When you go and buy your ticket
for the lottery Saturday night
and eight o'clock is fast approaching
and this time you're sure you've got it right
so you turn the television on
and they make the multimillion pound draw
then you discover that you've lost again
do you ever get the feeling
this has happened to you
Before

2
When you sit together at home at night
and the lights are turned down low
you're alone at last with the one you love
outside it's deep with snow
and it's not only the fire that's getting hot
but then a knock comes on the door
do you look at one another and say
do you ever get the feeling
this has happened to you
Before

3
When the whole season's biggest game
is being played by your team and another
and your team is leading by two goals
there's no way the opposition can recover
you start the victory celebrations
then suddenly they even up the score
but worse a third goes in and the game's been lost
do you ever get the feeling
this has happened to you
Before

4

When you go out to a friend's house
And you're doing all sorts of test
And the score is added up
and your mate's son comes out the best
and your mate comes second his wife third
and losing is something you deplore
and your wife comes fourth and you come last
do you ever get the feeling
this has happened to you
Before

5

I sat down one evening and decided
to write a poem about deja-vu
but l wasn't sure if I'd done so previously
it's the sort of thing that I might do
so I didn't bother writing it or send you a copy,
that would be a bore
if you received it, you'd only say to yourself
do you ever get the feeling
this has happened to me
Before

THE JERK
© Gordon martin

When you are in the pub with your mates
at the end of the day
and Parkinson's strikes, mobility's gone
and you hear some jerk say
Hey buddy, move over get your butt out the way
Let me tell you jerk
just how lucky you are
Any other time it would be
tag him and bag him and send
him home to his ma

The Cumberland
© Gordon martin

Kev is trying to double
the profits of Stella
you know you couldn't meet
a friendlier type of fella
Martin's beside him
in the number two berth
As people go
he's the salt of the earth
Diana's got her Mo - Geo working,
they're having a chat
about clothes jewellery and
people the week's events this and that
And it crosses my mind that
I ought to put down in prose
That the world would be a lot better
filled with friends such as those
So if you're ever downhearted
and need something to cheer
Pop down to the Cumberland
for friendship and beer

The Ghost
© Gordon martin

1

I guess I always saw this coming
I knew that deep inside
There was only ever one love in your life
And I can honestly say I tried
Go and start a new life
Where you can relax and rest
Even through all this tearful bitterness
I wish you all the best

2

I know you really cared for me
That I can't deny
You always did more than your share
I'm sorry I made you cry
All the things that I'm accused of
I guess guilty is the call
But none of these crimes were perpetrated
For any reason but the good of all

3

My master plan was always
To reach old age as best we could
And crazy though it's turned out
That's the ground on which I stood
And for all the faults on record
I never thought that you would leave
I now realize I never noticed
You wore your heart upon your sleeve

4
And you could look at me and say
that you always kept your pledge
And I could listen and never know
How close you wandered to the edge
Was it just a surrealist's displaced dream
Or a madman's crazy nightmare
Or was something best forgotten
From the world you left back there

5
So say goodbye, and start anew
But always remember this
I see your soul I feel your heart
I cherish your tender kiss
I carry the lie I know the truth
And deep inside you know it too
In life in death eternally
Its ghost will haunt both me and you

Nieces, Cathrine and Julia c.1994

Gordon's much loved Sister in law
Linda with husband Terry c. 1996

STRANGE DAYS
© Gordon martin

1
Diana's preparing a five course meal
We're getting the full job
Martin's off Mowtown music at the moment
He'd rather listen to Bob
Maureen's declined a shopping trip for clothes
She says there's nothing that I need
I think computers are one big bore
Strange days indeed

2
Martin's put a ban on watching boxing
" It's a brutal barbaric sport"
Maureen's turned down the chance to go away
"I'll only do it as a last resort"
Diana's campaigning for a ban on dogs
"l don't like that 'Bijon Frise' breed"
I'm trying to outlaw poetry
Strange days indeed

3
Maureen's giving up her sewing
She says it's giving her the stitch
Diana wants to ban Mystic Meg
She thinks that she's a witch
Martin's struggling to wire the plug up
On his television lead
I suggest that quizzes are a bore
Strange days indeed

CONVERSATION FOR TWO

© **Gordon martin 1994**

Everybody seems happy
The banqueting hall is packed
The feast is laid out before us
The wine is unracked
As the night draws on
The conversation's for two
And I sit holding my drink
And looking at you
But you're not sitting with me
You're with some other guy
And nothing exists
Beyond eye to eye
So l swallow deep
As the shadow consumes
And to avoid this black vision
I decide to switch rooms
But now thoughts fill my head
And that's even worse
As my mind plays tricks with me
And I start to curse
What made me come here
A deep rooted spark
A million to one chance
A shot in the dark
A hope against hope
It couldn't be true
An insane belief
That I could be with you
And I put my head round the door
And look across at the view
Of him laughing and joking
With his arm around you
So I decide enough is enough
And turn away and take flight
I'm out of the building

And consumed by the night
And the mood just keeps dropping
In fact it's now in free fall
My head is exploding
As I picture it all
But I still can't erase
Your face from my mind
Your beauty and smile
I've just left behind
And I promise myself
No matter how long it may take
You're going to be mine
Of that, make no mistake
And if I have the power
It's going to be soon
And the one that you're with
Can take his turn with the Moon

More Like Me
© Gordon martin 1994

1
I know you waited patiently for your turn
and it took an hour or two
I'll never forget your look of surprise
when the last tickets went to the group in front of you
After all they'd only just arrived
and blatantly jumped the queue
But why do you expect fair play from them
people are greedy through and through
I told you people act like that
You told me it couldn't be true

If only you could be more like me
And I could be more like you.

2
The moment that you show success
Creates a contradictory view
People praise you and put you on a pedestal
But they also start to knock you too
The bigger you get, the harder you fall
And the critics write their revue
They tell you you've got it coming
A well trod path it's nothing new

If only you could me more like me
And I could be more like you

3
But I know you see good in most everyone
Except for the doom laden crew
And your kind nature and belief in fair play
Nearly always gets you through
Perhaps I should take good for what it is
And in time it might accrue

Then others too might follow us
Who knows what it could lead to

If only you could be more like me
And the world could be more like you

Niece Julia with husband Simon and their
children Daniel, Matthew and Hannah

Maureen and Gordon with Godson Matthew, c. 1995

Love And Belief
© **Gordon martin**

1
Love deeper than your dark eyes
Heart pounding out a need
Belief stronger than these arms that hold you
All you have to do is follow my lead

2
You go back to the outlands
Where you once were queen amongst the men
And yesterday is today once more
Will you be as you were then

3
Love deeper than your dark eyes
Heart pounding out a plea
Belief stronger than these arms that hold you
All you have to do is listen to me

4
There's a stranger in the distance
There's another in your recent past
There's a question that can't be answered
Who was, is, or will be, the last

5
Love deeper than your dark eyes
Heart pounding out a request
Belief stronger than these arms that hold you
All I wanted was the best

6
So I took the beauty offered
And consumed it with avaricious appetite
Enjoying every moment, second, minute, and hour
In the hotel room that night

7
Love deeper than your dark eyes
Heart pounding out so rare
Belief stronger than these arms that hold you
All you have to do is show you care

8
Love deeper than my dark eyes
Heart pounding out a rhythmic beat
Belief stronger than these arms that hold you
The understanding is complete

****

Love - so freely given, so cheaply taken, so obviously misused, so often abused.
belief - so rarely committed, so often untried, one without the other just
perished and died
****

THERE IS LIFE OUT THERE!
© Gordon martin

WE FINALLY DISCOVERED LIFE IN SPACE

HUMAN JUST LIKE US

SO AN EXPEDITION WAS PROPOSED AND SENT

WITH THE MINIMUM OF FUSS

BUT AS WE LOOKED MORE CLOSELY

WE THOUGHT IT WOULD BE OF LITTLE WORTH

ALL THEY DID WAS FIGHT AND ARGUE

I THINK WE'LL STAY ON EARTH

MINE
© **Gordon martin**

Silently waiting
like lonely hearts do
I want you to come
so impatient for you
I've waited so long
I'm cold in my bed
I need your soft touch
to ignite my life thread

…I hear you approach...
....toward my direction

a union moments apart
an explosive connection

....a body,
…twisted and burnt

There's blood on the line
creating hell here on earth
the despicable land mine

no more to say!

****

Note
published in Poets for Peace
edited by David Foskett
Anchor books
#10.99
isbn 1 85930 039 1
****

THE MINUTE THAT WAS MAN
© Gordon martin

1
Days pass more quickly as you age
and history claims another year
Belief that life could be eternal
is washed away on death's first tear

2
The beauty of a new born life
The fury of inability to command
The solitude of inherited poverty
cling to the first outstretched and begging hand

3
So the battlefield is before us
The weapons left there we must choose
and use to survive, old age the prize
Don't even think that you may lose

4
The beauty of the victor's choice
The fury of the loser's pain
The solitude of the innocent
turn out to be one and the same

5
The unknown is waiting restlessly
The past is carried with regret
Both fight for our attention
but today is what matters yet

6
The beauty of that future hope
The fury of the deed you can't undo
The solitude when experience strangles innocence
The acceptance of the maturing you

7
The universe too vast to see
An eternity too long to size
A creation too magnificent to touch
The depth of a survivor's lonesome cry

8
The beauty of chaos redefined
The fury of nuclear fusion
The solitude of time and space
What is life and what an illusion?

9
We are born and soon departed
in a split-second of the master plan
In the book of endless ages
who will recall the minute that was man?

One Day
© Gordon martin

1
One lifetime might be wasted
one decade best forgot
one year passed without transgression
one summer was extremely hot

2
One month living with the family
one week spent alone away
one weekend that you had some fun once more
you know I'll make you mine:

one day!

****

Note
This is an anthem to anyone committed to be with someone they're not
I wonder how many people have this laying in some secret corner of their mind
****

New York
© Gordon martin

Gospel singers rhythmically singing praises to the Lord

Rappers rapping lyrics out like syncopated scores

Bag ladies shuffling to and fro about the corner of the street

They stay there because an extractor fan is pouring out some heat

Businessmen in pinstripe suits mix with yuppies on roller blades

As they head for work, meanwhile their wives go shopping in arcades

Central Park throws back the cloak it wore throughout the night

And with it go the ghost-men with unsatiated appetite

The streets are jamming early, there's gridlock 8 am

It was always going to be this way, the President's here again

Police, controlling traffic, whilst riding chestnut or bay steeds

Looking more like some misplaced cowboy from a novel you might read

Down at the Port Authority the buses are at hand

To carry blue waves of Giants fans into the Meadowland

I took that trip once, what a sight, as we entered the bus station

Down and outs on hospital trolleys, arms swollen with inflammation

Of bruised skin, caused by needles too often used, not even clean

Injecting death directly in their veins, what an awful scene.

Through a road tunnel to New Jersey and we're in another state,

"If you want to see the Giants in New York you'll have a long time to wait."

The hotel porter said, " there's a chance of finding a scalper there"

And suddenly one's behind us with two tickets he can 'spare'

$50 for two the deal is done and before we can ask the time of day

And turn to thank our supplier, he's gone, probably miles away.

Phoenix Cardinals meet the hosts, it turns out a one-sided match

The Giants posting 35 before battening down the hatch.

Back in the City it's getting late, we eat, and head for the sack

Inside the door seven locks to lock and protect us from attack

Laid there we hear gunshots and sirens wailing loud,

And shouting in the distance from some night time party crowd.

It's a crazy mesmerizing city and take it as read from me

It's a place you must go to experience, so much there to do and see

No more cosmopolitan place on Earth that have I ever found

Fascination from the top of the Empire State down to the underground

As I fly home I recall a vision of Liberty's torch jutting from the sand

From a futuristic film* I saw, yet still held high by her delicate hand

But New York gone, no more to be, buried by the annals of changing time,

Now that would be a tragedy and the city's most serious crime.

****
*one of the planet of the Apes

Go Giants - the author
Go Jets - his wife
As someone once remarked:
That surely is a marriage made in Heaven
****

Gordon the 'joker' as self styled "Gormless"
Gordon in his old football hat with sons Andrew
& David and nieces & nephews, Jonathan, Joy,
Rowena, & Ian together with Mum and Dad

Family group at Dad's 80th birthday November 1998.
Maureen, Derek, Gail, Gordon, with Dad and Mum.

Maureen and Gordon at one of his last public functions with
friends from Hickleton Hall at Doncaster Dome in 2006

THE PRIME MINISTERS REPLY TO A QUESTION
(what he said and what he meant)
© Gordon martin

We have the situation under control

things are getting out of hand

we anticipated trouble somewhere

we didn't think they had this planned

we are sending reinforcements

we underestimated the other side

there's every chance it will all die down

I wonder if we can stop the relentless tide

we notified our neighbours

the ones we usually ignore

they say they're right behind us

but how far back I can't be sure

There's really no need to panic

if you have transport get the hell out

I'll give way to the opposition leader

I hate the way he has to shout

Yes of course we'll keep you fully briefed

if you believe that you are crazy

And disclose all relevant facts of course

but delayed and only then hazy

I just received a note from my office

what the hell does this thing say

Please excuse me for a moment

if I get out I'm gone for the whole of the day

I'm pleased to say the news is good

I've managed to get away with it this time

The disturbance is now under control

I think I'll make protest a capital crime

So gentlemen any more questions

I could stay here all day long

No?- well thank you all sincerely

It's fun in the house when you're on song

EARTHQUAKE
© Gordon martin

WE WERE LIVING ON THE WEST COAST

WHEN THE EARTHQUAKE HIT ONE DAY

AND THE RUMBLE AND THE ROAR HAD PASSED

BEFORE THE PRIEST HAD TIME TO PRAY

FOR LENIENCY AND MERCY

FOR EXCLUSION FROM THE TROUBLE

AND AS HE KNELT TO START TO PRAY

WAS HIT BY TWENTY TONS OF RUBBLE

THAT ONCE WAS A BEAUTIFUL CREATION

A MAGNIFICENT STEEPLE AND BELL

NOW JUST ONE MORE BUILDING, FALLING

AND POUNDING ITS INHABITANTS NEARER HELL.

WHEN THE SHAKING FINALLY STOPPED FOR GOOD

FROM THE QUAKE AND SEVERAL AFTERSHOCKS

NOTHING MUCH WAS MOVING

EXCEPT SOME TORN FREE FALLING ROCKS

ROLLING DOWN THE HILLSIDE

AND NOTHING MUCH WAS MAKING A SOUND

JUST THE TICKING OF THE CLOCK

COUNTING OUT IN SECONDS

WHAT SEEMED TO LAST FOR HOURS

AND DOGS RAN CRAZY WITH CONFUSION

RAN THROUGH A CONTRADICTORY VISION

OF BURNING BUILDINGS SET ALIGHT BY POWER

FROM PYLON'S WIRES JUST CUT LIKE THREAD

AND GUSHING WATER SPRAYING EVERYWHERE

FROM PIPES EJECTED FROM THEIR SHALLOW BED

NO CONTEST FOR THE EARTH'S INSISTENCE

ON SHOWING MAN'S ABILITY TO CONQUER NATURE

AS NOTHING MORE THAN INSUFFICENT PETTY POOR
RESISTANCE

SMART, SMARTER, SMARTEST
© **Gordon martin**

The election is set, the buses and gravy trains are rolling, and the parties are squaring up to each other.

Of course we should vote for the party with what we consider to be the best policies, at least, if not for the United Kingdom, then for ourselves. This is not as unpatriotic as it might first appear. History is scattered with politicians, whose only purpose in life was to get out of it whatever they could for themselves.

Which brings me to my point. Perhaps we should vote for the party or its leader that is the smartest, not necessarily academically, for we all know irrespective of our schooling, that the world is not led or won by the university elite. And thankful for the fact, we should be too.

So who is smart, who is smarter, and who is smartest.

So far, my vote for smart goes to Paddy Ashdown.
Tough luck Paddy, that leaves you in third place. He is smart because he is playing it down the line, just as he sees it, or when blinded, following the appropriate opposition policy for the ride.

If he sees more votes in the Labour option,
let's call it Concorde, he gets on.

If he doesn't like the Tory option, let's call it airbus, he doesn't.

Just hope he sees the Titanic for what it is, when he gets the invitation to sail.

Smarter and therefore runner up is John Major.
Nice ploy that, John.

When the chance of going head to head with Tony came along, you just had to point out that the Liberals weren't a real party, thus ensuring that you got the backs up of all the lemonheads, and thereby effectively keeping the opposition vote split.

Smarter, but not smart enough.

The current leader, and I must admit it, this one nearly fooled me, is..........
Tony Blair.

Yes he came up with a wonderful tactic, when he got his own man to put himself out of a job for the next five years, convincing him to let Martin Bell, stand as the anti-sleaze candidate. Stupid you say!

Not so!

In one swoop, Tony has diverted all the Tory spin doctors off himself and onto this poor news reporter.

While they are busy trying to find mud to sling at Martin, Tony gets on with the clean cut style.

Well? Have you seen a photo-opportunity with the two of them together?

Me neither.

Smartest?

Tony!!

SPANISH DAYS
© **Gordon martin**

1
Walking on the beach one night
I saw a Spanish lad on the sands
two Skye terriers running around his legs
two leashes in his hands
and both those terriers were wearing
bandanas tied loosely round their necks
the grey dog red with white spots on
the black dog's blue and silver check

Chorus
And out at sea a seagull cried
and the fisherman's light flicked on
and the waves rolled in relentlessly
and the stars in the Spanish sky shone

2
The sun beats down on the harbour
where the fishermen mend their trawl
and offload the catch for market
just another day that's all
for every day the sun comes up
and with it come the fishermen
and as evening comes and the sun goes down
out go the fishermen once again

Chorus
And out at sea a seagull cried
And the fisherman's light flicked on
And the waves rolled in relentlessly
And the stars in the Spanish sky shone

3

Walking on the beach next night
I saw two lovers looking out to sea
and talking to each other
they didn't even notice me
and both the lovers wore a smile
that showed an understanding
that love is kind and gentle
not commanding or demanding

Chorus
And out at sea a seagull cried
and the fisherman's light flicked on
and the waves rolled in relentlessly
and the stars in the Spanish sky shone

4

Walking on the beach tonight
before I pack my bags and go
I thought about the Spanish lad
and how he loved the terriers so
and I thought about the lovers
and in my mind I said a prayer
May they have their love continue and grow
just as the love my lady and I now share

Chorus
And out at sea a seagull cried
And a tear dropped from my eye
And the waves rolled in relentlessly
And I bade the starry Spanish sky goodbye

STEEL CITY
© **Gordon martin**

1
No more the blackened sooty sky
that made strong men cough and children cry
No more a hammering no more a cage
that dropped a man to a mile deep grave
No Sunday school singing ' Jerusalem'
no more homecoming hob-nailed booted men
No more the woman on leaded step sat
no more the scratching of bubonic rat
No more the gas lamp's uneven fight
against shadowy terraces black as night
No more the early morning call
to long hours of work for nothing at all

2
Instead a new environmental dream
a cleaner and more pleasant green
A brighter city, modern too
with malls and cinemas there for you
But with the passing of the steel
went the jobs, part of the deal
So who will relish this brave new world
an advertiser's dream, with flags unfurled
The industrial lot now done by machine
no workmen needed in this scene
Yet just one thought for an idle nation,
Will machines be taught to buy their own creations?

SILENT CONTEMPLATION
© **Gordon martin**

I never realized that silence had so many different keys
A multitude of complications and variations on a theme
Sat at the grand piano in the corner of the room
In silent contemplation her thoughts in syncopated tune
She's pretty but not demanding, the piano does not need to play a
song
There's symmetrical counterpunching melody in silence impossible
to play wrong
The artist capturing in perfect harmony the beauty of silence peace
and calm
In monochromatic silent contemplation a picture welcoming and
warm

****

Note
These untitled lines were found after Gordon's death. We have given its title
because we believe they are a description of a favourite painting of his by
Mark Spain, called Silent Contemplation, painted in sepia, and depicting a
girl beside a piano keyboard,

****

THE BOOK
© Gordon martin

1
He sits watching the ships on the horizon
She's reading a paperback romance
He thinks of his home back in England
She dines with a playboy from France

2
He says ' Are you enjoying the sanctuary?'
She says 'yes', but her eyes don't look up
He pours a beer into an old glass tumbler
She drinks Earl Grey from a fine china cup

3
He wonders where the ships have set sail for.
She kisses a handsome young face.
"Bound for England." he thinks, as he watches.
She's thinking only of satin and lace.

4
He asks ' Are you anything wanting?"
She says 'no' and continually reads on
When a man bursts into the room,
With a pistol, one shot and her lover is gone

5
A tear drops on the last page of the booklet
A story ends with distressing surprise
'Why the tear, my love, what saddens?'
'A man I've known all his life has just died.'

6
'Who is this man that you mention?
Do I know him and is he a threat?'
'Oh no, he's just a man in a story' she says
.........But the page of the book is still wet!

****

Note
On holiday my wife is prone to sudden outbursts of tears, usually by a
crowded swimming pool. This explains why!
****

The Resistance
© **Gordon martin**

1
We met as arranged at the siding
after we had been to see Yvette
who told us where our comrades were
and quietly fixed our bayonet
we dropped down the hillside where
we set off vivid bright flares,
to confuse those sleeping there
turning peaceful dreams to a waking nightmare

2
All the enemy were killed that night
either by bayonet, bullet or blade
and the priest there with us prayed for their souls
and a plea for God's mercy was made.
And as we looked all around
we swore you could hear the sound
of wailing coming up through the ground
and the cackling laugh of the devil abound

****

Note
Did they think they were right?
****

THINGS ARE DIFFERENT (IT WAS ALWAYS GOING TO BE)
© **Gordon martin**

1
I don't get over as often as I did before
But I guess we always knew the score
You don't have the time to make that call
It's not your fault
Things are different that's all

2
The situation has been revised
Why should you look so mystified
It was always going to be this way
Don't say you never realised

3
I could say I miss the old connection
We had the choice of acceptance or rejection
You could say your back's against the wall
It's not your fault
Things are different that's all

4
The position has been redefined,
It's been unfair, but life was never kind
It was always going to be this way.
Don't say it's burning up your mind

5
I wish we could retrace the whole event
But you either volunteer are called, or sent.
You could walk away, and I could crawl,
It's not your fault ,
Things are different, that's all.

****

These verses have been set to music and recorded by
Kevin Fitzpatrick
And were sung by Kevin at Gordon's funeral
****

The Trawler
(A Story In Five Parts)
© **Gordon martin**

part one
LOVE FOR THE SEA

1

He was just another kid from the city,
Hard worker, good looker, very serious and gritty.
Never left the high rise, cold grey, council towers.
Never had a minute to think, though it usually took hours.
Always at the car factory fifteen minutes before due.
Welded chassis together black, silver and blue.
Never once took his mind off the work that he did,
He took pride in that fact, a real likable kid.

2

She worked in the florists, at the corner of town,
And when she finished her day, and the shop was closed down,
She went to the pub, where he told her to wait,
In the skyscraper, concreted jungle estate.
They were out of this town, they were heading south west,
They'd been told that the climate down there was the best.
Down to the coast where the sailors all sat,
Discussing past journeys, old times, this and that.

3

Of days when they travelled, so far, out from land,
That the sea was in view, no matter which aspect was scanned.
Of how they clung to the riggings, when a storm tossed the boat,
And the swell lifted and dropped it, but it still kept afloat.
When lightning struck fear into the hearts of the crew,
Whether timid or brave as the dark storm clouds grew,
And how it taught them respect, for every man on the craft,
And when it was over how they drank, joked and laughed.

4
They had always remarked how strange life could be,
When your life hangs by a thread when in peril at sea,
Held by the man next to you when you haul in the trawl,
Or by the hand of the Master that created us all.
Would they stand another destructive electrical fork,
As the storm in its rage, tossed the boat like a cork.
One thing was certain, call it mad or insane,
But their love for the sea would send them out there again.

THE TRAWLER

part two
THE ARRIVAL AT PORT

5

But to continue my story, the Captain was looking to hire
As the eldest crew member was convinced to retire.
So when the kid from the city drove in through the chine,
He was happy to see the job vacancy sign,
And within minutes was talking to the Captain in dock,
Who said Be here, this evening at about eight o'clock.
We set sail at ten, and you'll find the work rough,
But I think you'll survive, if you're honest and tough.

6

Then with his girl, made his way to a cobbled side street,
Where he and their landlord had arranged earlier to meet.
After agreeing to rent the cottage looking out toward sea
They unpacked the car and were without doubt carefree.
He could see the men from the window working away
Preparing the nets for the trawl later that day
When he would be with them as the sun slowly set
And by the light of the moon would be working the net

7

Now she too is making plans for a house no more a dream
But they'd do it together like any good team
Soon evening was here and as he walked out of sight
She waved and shouted aloud "Darling take care tonight"
But her thoughts were 'tomorrow I'll tell him the news,
And ask him some names that he might like to choose.'
For the doctor confirmed what they had long talked about
A baby they wanted no longer a doubt

8
He arrived at the quayside at seven forty three
And with the rest of crew, prepared the boat for the sea.
He was put with a man who had spent years on the trawl,
And if you needed experience, then he had it all.
The Captain was practical, he wanted a good trip,
He would never let a novice work alone on the ship.
He prided himself that over the years,
He never lost a man, nor saw a widow in tears.

THE TRAWLER

part three
OUT AT SEA

9
So now, some hours later, they're miles off the coast
The night is pitch black, the way they like it the most.
The trawler can trawl, alone and unseen
And take the catch that it wants, no-one knows where they've been
And discharge their catch back at port early dawn,
While the cock still crows the morn.
The Captain gives orders to the men on the deck,
Work like the devil tonight, or I'll have your tough neck.

10
Back at the house, the girl headed for bed,
But found sleeping impossible, when she laid down her head.
Her thoughts were of him, and the vast ocean wide,
And the freezing cold night, and as she lay there she cried.
Cried a mixture of happiness and sadness as one,
A new home to live in, but her lover now gone,
Burning his hands as the trawl net sped through,
On a boat out at sea and the storm breaking too.

11
Later that night, the storm pounded the coast,
It was the one thing the girl, in her thoughts, feared the most.
The storm was the worst anyone could recall,
Even the man who retired, and he'd seen them all.
Strange thoughts crossed her mind, as she laid there in bed
All she could see was a black cloud overhead,
And a boat battered, beleaguered and twisted in form,
And the men thrown about by the strength of the storm

12
She was out of bed, dressed, and in a raincoat,
Making her way to the harbour to wait for the boat.
Other women, some men, but few children were there,
Their faces frozen and wet each one wearing a stare.
Then someone caught sight on the horizon south east,
Of a speck, yes, the boat! and a cheer was released.
There was relief to those waiting as familiar faces appeared
But no sign of her love even as the boat neared

THE TRAWLER

part four
THE DISASTER

13
Then a strange thing occurred to the crowd on the land
Not one sailor was smiling nor waving his hand
Silence spread quickly round those stood in port
As they waited for the Captain to disembark and report,
And the Captain first off made straight for the girl.
His face told the story, her head started to whirl.
With tears in his eyes, "I must tell you," he said
"A man was lost overboard, the one you love is presumed dead!"

14
Though foreseen, the shock hit her nevertheless,
And she dropped to the floor, in a instant, I guess,
Overcome by the grief of the message imparted,
Only twenty four hours after their new life had started.
When she came round, she was sat in a chair
In the Harbourmaster's office, two men were stood there.
The Harbourmaster's face had a kind, sorry look,
The Captain was writing the night's events in a book.

15
"Can it be true, Captain, what you have just said to me.
Does my love lay cold under the dark desolate sea?"
"I'm sorry to tell you as we hauled in the net
A jig broke, there was panic, but though it was wet
Your love held on to the rope that was slipping away
Many a good sailor couldn't do that even today
His hands were bleeding from friction burns still
He wouldn't let go in that cold icy chill

16
And as the storm tossed the boat again and again
He was thrown overboard to the despair of the men
And there's a lifeboat out there now searching the sea
Carrying the hopes of all, God, you and me
We wait now for news" - and as he uttered the word
A signal on the radio from the lifeboat was heard
Lifeboat calling base Code Five
We've recovered a body though barely alive

THE TRAWLER

part five
EPILOGUE

So……..

17
The thought that would be raised many more times yet
Was again in the heads, of those, that to live, cast a net.
Will he survive, his life thread held by the One who created us all
Or will the bony black finger of the devil let it fall?
She prayed that he would return home, still breathing and quick,
And looked only to sea as the clock continued to tick.
Finally, the life boat arrived, the Skipper's face all aglow
And that in itself told her what she wanted to know.

18
Two days later, he was out of intensive care,
And another week on, you couldn't find him in there.
He continued to live a life out at sea,
And the baby boy born, made a family of three.
When they chose a name for their son, they needed no vote,
He was named after the Skipper of the heroic lifeboat
And I can tell you for certain, this story is true,

That man was my father …

…it's the son talking to you!

****
Note
for those in peril out at sea
BRAVE men one and all
****

WALK ALONE
©Gordon martin

1
Once days were like an endless summer
But we never quite closed the door
Whatever we had, you rearranged
As much as offered, you wanted more
There's a thousand ghosts around you
Some mysterious some well known

But beside me there is no-one
Because of you I walk alone

2
Oh the laurel trees form patterns
That surrealists find a bore
And just like the clear fresh morning
I just want you more and more
Relationships with time have grown
With a lingering soulful tone

But as I look around me
Because of you I walk alone

3
I've told you many times I love you
You can't deny the score
I'm living in a vacuum scene where
My dreams wash up on a distant shore
My heartbeat is still passion bent
Not dead like a bloodless stone

Just listen and you will hear it
Because of you I walk alone

WHEN
© Gordon martin

1
WHEN THE ARABS HAVE SPENT ALL THEIR MONEY
WHEN THE THAMES FLOWS INTO THE RIVER SEINE
WHEN CANTONA CAN'T PASS OR SHOOT
WHEN AMERICA IS UNDER BRITISH RULE AGAIN
THAT'S WHEN,
AND ONLY MAYBE THEN..
I TELL YOU THAT WE'RE THROUGH
AND I GIVE UP ON YOU.

2
WHEN BOB CAN'T WRITE A LYRIC WITH MEANING
WHEN POLITICANS DEBATE WITHOUT COMMOTION
WHEN WIMBLEDON CAN'T STAGE A TENNIS MATCH
WHEN ATLANTIS RISES FROM THE OCEAN
THAT'S WHEN,
AND ONLY MAYBE THEN..
I TELL YOU THAT WE'RE THROUGH
AND I GIVE UP ON YOU.

3
WHEN THE SECOND COMING IS AT HAND
AND THE APOCALYPSE HAS STARTED
WHEN THE DEVIL TEARS MY HEART FROM ME
WHEN MY LAST BREATH FROM BODY HAS DEPARTED
THAT'S WHEN,
AND ONLY MAYBE THEN..
I TELL YOU THAT WE'RE THROUGH
AND I GIVE UP ON YOU.

4
WHEN THEY FIND INTELLIGENCE IN OUTER SPACE
WHEN A YEAR ENDS FREE FROM MAJOR DISASTER
WHEN WE SCOOP THE LOTTERY THREE TIMES
STRAIGHT

THE WORLD ENDS AND THERE'S NO HEREAFTER
THAT'S WHEN,
AND ONLY MAYBE THEN..

you've seen all that there is to see
and you finally give up on me

5
ANOTHER DAY YOU TRIED
ANOTHER DAY YOU SURVIVED
TAKE PRIDE!

****
Looking back it's hard to pinpoint a time when I meant less to you
The time when you turned your collar up to the cold winds of indifference
When you decided that others were more important
Whatever I offered it was never quite enough
The ghosts of previous times and there were many of them
Shrieked and spun round my brain causing me to be temporarily insane
Did someone spark a reaction or were you taken down the road of trials
To the raging torrent, All the ambition that was swept away on the river of selfishness
And all the dreams that got tangled up in the weeds of uncertainty
We had it all and we watched and let it drift aimlessly out of sight
****

WORLD WAR III
© **Gordon martin**

Once there was a stack of charter planes,

circling as they wait their turn to land,

and disgorge the shorts and T-shirt tourists,

with their radios in their hands.

Now, there's just a runway,

and a fuel dump, and some fighters,

and a curfew on the nightclubs,

that used to stage the long all nighters.

The world gets instant horror

from satellite dishes in neat rows,

on sand that once you couldn't move on,

but now where no-one ever goes.

There's desolation in the city parks,

where the children used to play.

The hotels are full of news reporters,

where the tourists used to stay.

One CNN reporter says

''I was about to grab a bite to eat,

when I looked out of the window,

and saw a missile heading down the street!"

It's an anaesthetised emotion,

you have with instant news,

when you listen to an interview,

of a dictator's cleverly worded views.

But the reality is not in T.V. studios,

it's out there, in the front line.

It's a refugee at eighty four

It's a child of five,

stepping on a mine!

It's a motherless baby, left crying,

it's a hospital, awash with blood,

it's ten surgeons, trying to save a thousand lives,

it's bodies trampled in the mud.

You just can't work it out at all,

why people and countries fight,

why they can't all live together,

and sleep safely in their beds at night.

Why people can't have a different religion,

or belief that they stand for,

without pursuing it to the insane extent,

of the eve of a THIRD WORLD WAR?

****
Note:
for all the greedy, conceited, egotistic 'leaders'
who feed on aggression in the world today.......
....and when you die - hell roast you
******

published in poets for peace edited by David Foskett anchor books
#10.99 ISBN 1 85930 039 1
****

WOLVES
© Gordon martin

WHEN TIME PASSES BY AND YOU'RE NOT YOUNG
ANYMORE
WHEN YOU LOOK FOR THE WOLVERHAMPTON
WANDERERS SCORE
AND FOR A MOMENT YOU'RE HAPPY 'COS THEY
KNOCKED IN TWO
BUT THEN THE OTHERS GOT FOUR AND YOU FEEL SO
BLUE
AND YOU RING YOUR MATE BUT HE'S ON THE LINE
AND YOUR WIFE'S JUST OPENED ANOTHER BOTTLE OF
WINE
AND YOU THINK BACK TO THE DAYS WHEN THE
WOLVES HAD A SCHEME

AND THE OLD GOLD AND BLACK WAS A WINNING
DREAM TEAM
WHEN WAGSTAFFE WOULD RACE STRAIGHT AWAY
DOWN THE WING
AND DROP IT ON THE HEAD OF THE DOOG AS FANS
SING
'WHAT'S HIS NAME' THE REPLY 'DOUGAN' WAS JOYFULLY
CHANTED
AS INTO THE GOAL THE KNOCKED DOWN BALL HAD
BEEN SLANTED

THEN YOUR MIND SNAPS BACK TO THE PRESENT TIME
AND YOU'RE THINKING THERE'S NO REASON OR RHYME
SO YOU TRY YOUR MATE AGAIN BUT THE PHONE'S STILL
ENGAGED
BUT YOU NEED TO TALK SOON 'COS YOU'RE SO
ENRAGED
GOOD GOD IS THERE NO ONE TO SYMPATHISE
WHO SEES THE SAME GAME AS YOU BUT THROUGH HIS
OWN EYES

AND AS YOU CONSIDER YOU HEAR SOMEONE SNORING
AND YOUR WIFE'S FAST ASLEEP - IS WINE REALLY THAT
BORING
NOW YOUR BRAIN IS ERUPTING YOUR FEVER IS HOT
SO YOU PICK UP THE PHONE AND GIVE YOUR MATE
ONE MORE SHOT
AND THE LINE CONNECTS THROUGH AND YOU GIVE
YOUR TEAM HELL
AND THERE'S A DEATHLY HUSH BUT WHY IS DIFFICULT
TO TELL

AND YOU HEAR YOUR MATE SWALLOW HARD EVEN
THOUGH WELL OUT OF RANGE
AS HE MUTTERS
WELL I THOUGHT THEY PLAYED PRETTY GOOD FOR A
CHANGE

(Written by) GORDON MARTIN A LONG SUFFERING FAN
(for his equally long suffering Mate Mick!)

GHOSTS OF YESTERDAY
© **Gordon martin**

Here and there some pictures
are hanging from the wall
or filling an empty window sill
or decorating the entrance hall
pictures of a bygone day
in sepia or black and white
of soldiers long forgotten
except by friends that stood to fight
alongside these soulless images
just paper on a wall
not blood or mud or bullet wound
not trench or gas or cannon ball.
As the evening draws its curfew
on the daylight's yellow ray
and the colours of the planet Earth
turn a million shades of grey
the echoes of those yesterdays
hang like ether in the air
you can't see them touch them smell them
but somehow you know they're there
and when darkness finally takes control
and rearranges all your senses
that very essence permeates your brain
and heart beats faster and muscle tenses
it's then the ghosts of yesterday begin
to helter skelter through your brain
and confusion conquers logic
and you're temporarily insane
and just as the madness seems as though
it's about to burst your head
thinking of tragedies that once befell you
and those you loved but long since dead
a crack of light breaks on the horizon
and the first sunlight looks your way
and you rub your eyes to wake you
and you're thankful for the day

The Black And White Rainbow

© **Gordon martin**

1

Every day seems like rain
there's been no sun for a week
it's hard waking alone
and not hearing you speak
There's a black and white rainbow
in a colourless sky
and an aching inside
since you told me goodbye

2

I look out of the window
hoping for the warmth of the day
but the sky's just been rain and more rain
since you went far away
and the rainbow stays there
like piano keys in the sky
playing a dirge to remind me
you told me goodbye

3

I go out for a walk
to the park where we met
but there's no sign of it easing
less it stopping just yet
and I sit on the bench
where we sat eye to eye
and the rainbow before me reminds me
you told me goodbye

4

Then the temperature drops
and the rain turns to snow
but the black and white rainbow
refuses to go

and now it's like crows circling around
in the white whispery sky
Waiting to peck on my misery
since you told me goodbye

5
So I make my way back home
and the rainbow's always in view
like a white ghost in the night
to remind me of you
and as I turn the street corner
my eyes are hit with the sight
of the most beautiful rainbow
kaleidoscope light

6
And you're standing there smiling
And waiting for me
And the black and white rainbow
Will I never again see

AMERICA
© Gordon martin

(Verse in five parts)
PART 1

America cannot be defined by text books television or tourists.
America is millions of people each believing they are what America
is.... and they are.
From the man that walked on the moon, to the man that never left a
pool room.
From the man that leads the nation to the woman that first loved
him.
From the vast plains' farmer to the city dude to the beach bar
attendant on the sun coast.
All believe they are America... and they are.
For America is so complex, you have eat, breath, smell and taste it.
And feel it.
Let it ooze into your conscience.
Let it flow through your blood.
Let it permeate your brain.
It is everything you hoped it might be..... and more.
It is everything you couldn't believe it was portrayed to be.... and
more.
The man that wouldn't drink with another will stand shoulder to
shoulder with him under its flag.
If you were to define single-mindedness, then America
is it.
They truly believe they have created the home of the brave and
the land of the free, yet complain about all and sundry miniscular
subjects.
There is nothing they don't have an opinion on.
If you want America to be cheap it is.
If you want America to be opulent it is.
If you want America to exude fair play it will.
If you want America to be corrupt it can be.
If you want to travel a mile in America it will provide you with a taxi,
a shuttle or an automatic walkway, but it may not offer you a path.
If you like sport there many channels each day providing it and they

are World Champions at all their sports...but no-one else plays them.
When you buy a newspaper you get a rain forest .
Page upon page of local trivia, shopping and national news.... but
does the rest of the world exist?
If it does it doesn't concern the media. There is little or no news from
abroad.
You don't shop in shops, you shop in Malls, that rise amongst the
criss-cross grid that is a perfect road system, like a new Atlantis rising
from the ocean.
And women are drawn to them mesmerised by the sparkling purity
of it all, a smile appearing on their faces even as they near the great
monoliths that say "this is the American dream and you can have it."
You are sucked into the entrepreneurs whirlpool , reconditioned , and
sent home a different person.
And you wonder how you managed without the things that you
purchased.
And you love America ...
and it loves you.
It takes your money and gives you what you want.
And what's wrong with that.
Long may it continue.

PART 2

America is steam rising from the manholes in a New York street.
America is a burst fire hydrant spraying water on the sidewalk.
America is a beach boardwalk that leads to a bar you wouldn't be seen
dead in but where in America it has a charm of its own.
Young tugs and fast cars.
Pretty girls and bikinis.
A hundred varieties of beer all sold in this few square yards on the
beach overlooking the Gulf of Mexico.
We are sitting there one night when a guy rolls up, literally, in a
wheelchair. He's about twenty one, has great looks, long blonde
ragged hair down to his shoulders, and a bronzed body.
But he is paralysed from the waist down.
His legs are wasted.
He tells us one night he thumbed a lift home in a pickup van
and as it turned into McDonalds was hit at eighty five mph by an
oncoming car, the driver drunk.
He took the brunt of the collision.
He bums a cigarette off two pretty girls at the bar.
We continue to talk.
I tell him of my Parkinsonism .
I feel sorry for him and him for me.
We shake hands.
A shake that says we are brothers of fate.
A shake that says isn't life tough, but you have to get on with it.
A shake that says Respect.
And he turns into the night and is gone..

PART 3

America is baseball cards.

Baseball cards that sell for two cents or twenty thousand dollars.

When they had a problem with pilfering of packets, what did they do?

Move them nearer the counter - didn't work.

So someone came up with the idea of putting them in tins.

So now you buy canned baseball cards.

America is the only country you can be void of any intelligence and still get a scholarship. For in America if you can play sport, and this definition includes putting on as much bulk as you can and standing in front of a quarterback to protect him while a similar guy on the other side tries to get past you by putting your head in your feet, you can go to college.

America is where soft ice cream is called custard, your bum is your fanny and crisps are chips, chips are fries.

America is where you drive in almost anywhere - cinema food bank whatever.

You never need to leave your car.

Car? - I've seen smaller armoured vehicles.

These aren't classic, they are a work of art.

I wonder what a mini would actually look like parked next to a stretch limo.

I suppose about the same as England parked next to America

PART 4

America is a country where you can't go fifty yards without seeing
the stars and stripes. Banks, public buildings, professional businesses,
gas stations, liquor stores and gun shops. All fly the flag. Because
they are all proud to be American.. You may be Catholic, Protestant,
Mormon, Hindu or Jesuit. You may be Irish, Puerto Rican, Cuban,
or Canadian by descent. You may admire Thatcher, Che Guevara,
Hitler or Mao Tse Tung. You may be affiliated to Greenpeace, Sinn
Fein or Black Power. But whatever you are still American.
The allegiance to the flag is impressive. Before sports games , at
school, at public meetings.
And their anthem actually means something.
Oh say can you see through the dawn's early light,
What so proudly we hailed at the twilight's last fading
and the tune is stirring, it gets hold of you and wrenches your
emotions.
It is however very difficult to sing, and many a professed singer has
floundered publicly attempting to do so.
America is the land of the great white hope - the belief that a
white American will once again become the World Heavyweight
Champion, yet many quarters still fail to recognize the greatest of
them all - Mohammed Ali.
America is the country where an overseas boxer has to knock out an
American to draw.
If America feels the need to do something, it will.
Go to the moon.
Have a witch-hunt on Communists.
Form the Ku Klux Klan.
Send troops to Vietnam.
There is nothing you can't get in America, that you can elsewhere.
Plastic Surgery more advanced than the Space programme.
T V Shows of psychoanalysis of every misfortune, malady and
misdemeanour, that intersperse with the most banal quiz shows.
People willing to go on national television and expose their family
misfortunes for a quick buck.
For in America cash (or at least plastic cash) is king.

Recently America had a string of terrorist activity.
America was surprised.
America believing that everyone in America was American, couldn't
comprehend it.
After all you don't blow your own house up, or shoot your brother.
So as long as they kept strict control on immigration, it wouldn't -
couldn't - happen.
BANG.
Hello America. This is what it's like when you send money to Ireland.
BANG.
Innocent victims suffer as they do worldwide.
So would America Apprehend the culprits?
You have to say their detection rate is superb
..........or...............

PART 5

You may be wondering by now whether I like America.
I Love It.
But America needs to realize the world doesn't end at Anchorage,
Atlantic City or Los Angeles.
America is bigger and better, classier and cheaper, smarter and
sunnier,
friendlier and funnier, but it can be darker and deadlier too.
As they said in the Trojan war - never look a gift horse in the mouth.
Respect America and it will respect you.
Love America and it will love you.
Take America for granted and it will take you..
for granted
for a fool
for all your cash
for no other reason than you underestimated it.

Hope to be back there soon!!

****
Note:
Sadly Gordon was never to make the journey again
****

ANTIMATTER EXPLAINED
© Gordon martin

In the place of permanent present
Where time hasn't been conceived
the past has never happened
or the future been received
there a feeling of contentment
everything as is for sure
nothing getting better or worse
just the same for evermore

Eternity becomes a concept
explained in one dimension
and salvation has no meaning
when change is outside comprehension
but to get there you need to be reborn
when the chance comes along one day
just drop into anti matter
when a black hole passes by your way

GOD AND EINSTEIN
© Gordon martin

1
Mother nurtures baby
Sailor out at sea
Pauper in the hostel bed
Murderers set free
President on the podium
Security wherever he wants to go
Evolution or Confusion
Only God and Einstein know

2
Russia is in turmoil
Tiger in decline
Monarchy in disarray
Was water really turned to wine
Giggs is flying down the wing
Gates is buying Singapore
Making multimillion profits
Only God and Einstein can keep score

3
Plague wipes out seventy thousand
The Great War takes eight million lives
Still Africa is too populous
Even though starvation thrives
Power is an aphrodisiac
Money talks a language plain
Religion is a cult to some
Only God and Einstein can explain

4
Mist on the horizon
Darkness overhead
Eerie silence in the air
A man crucified 'til dead

Short life you led my Brother
To give us chance to live
Were the nails you took worthwhile
An answer God alone can give

DIANA
PRINCESS OF WALES
QUEEN OF HEARTS
© Gordon martin

When the last tear has finally been cried
When the last broken heart been mended
When the good you did is forgotten or denied
Is the day this crazy world has ended

Your maturity in innocence
your sophistication of the simple life
your wisdom with a common touch
your tranquillity in strife
your beauty in an ugly world
your calming influence of man's rage
your kindness in aggressive times
your sincerity in a ruthless age
All these will be remembered
of you, Diana, Queen of Hearts,
The humanitarian, the lady,
Gone, but now the legend starts

If as we are told by some
that beauty is truly only to be found skin deep
then the beauty of Diana
Is for her friends and family to keep
But if beauty is in reality
from inside and from the heart
then the beauty of Diana
is shared by everyone in equal part

A Lesson Learnt
© Gordon martin

1
Taking time to give protection
to the morals of the rich.
Call it protocol or tradition
it doesn't matter which
Either way it's just a reason
to continue to control
But in the end your life is nothing
if you don't recognize your soul

2
People worldwide in their millions
without the luxury of choice
As individuals and in unison
came together in one voice
speaking words of sense and wisdom
Like a brother deep in pain
Look and learn from what's before you
and never let it happen again
your kindness in aggressive times
your sincerity in a ruthless age
All these will be remembered
of you, Diana, Queen of Hearts,
The humanitarian, the lady,
Gone, but now the legend starts

3
If as we are told by some
that beauty is truly only to be found skin deep
then the beauty of Diana
Is for her friends and family to keep
But if beauty is in reality
from inside and from the heart
then the beauty of Diana
is shared by everyone in equal part

In Memoriam

237

DIANA
© Gordon martin

Your children will age past you
Your brother and sisters will outlast you
Your friends grow old and grey
But you will always be remembered
In youthfulness and beauty

On Celebrating My Parents' Golden Wedding Anniversary
Lily And Gordon Martin
9th august 1994.
© Gordon martin

Golden thoughts, golden schemes
golden days, golden dreams
on this day, special to you
fifty years are in revue
days of laughter, days of tears
flood your memory, as you roll back the years
can it be, so long ago
you stood together, toe to toe
made a vow, to be joined forever
kissed and imagined the future together
then the years rolled by, where have they gone?
and the memories mounted, as time marched on
you still recall, each step of the way
as now together, you review this day
enjoy the moment, with family and friends
then as you sit together as the celebrations end
take a moment together, alone, to say
I'm glad I married you on that day
golden after
golden before
golden now and evermore

GOT WHAT I WANT
© Gordon martin

1
GOT A FEW POUNDS INSIDE MY SHIRT POCKET
GOT A FEW DREAMS BOTH OLD AND NEW
WANT A GOOD LAUGH AND A GOOD TIME BABY
HOW ABOUT IT ME AND YOU

2
GOT A LOT OF PATIENCE AND I NEED IT
GOT SOME IDEAS TO THROW AROUND
WANT TO SEE YOU LOOKING DOWN ON ME BABY
IF I'M EVER ON THE GROUND

3
GOT SOME LOVE BEEN SAVING FOR SHARING
GOT SOME THOUGHTS ON ETERNITY
WANT GOOD LOVE AND A GOOD WOMAN BABY
HOW ABOUT IT YOU AND ME

4
GOT TO GO NOW BABY COME WITH ME
TEACH YOU ALL ABOUT ECSTASY
I KNOW YOU'VE SUFFERED INJUSTICE BABY
BUT AT LEAST IT SET YOU FREE

5
GOT A REAL FEELIN THINGS ARE HAPP'NING
GOT MY MIND ON THAT WEDDING TROTH
WANT YOU ALL FOR MYSELF, ALONE , FOREVER
HOW 'BOUT IT YOU AND ME BOTH

THE HOUSE ON THE HILL NEAR GOLDEN BAY
© Gordon martin

1
The air is filled with expectation.
A hush settles now everyone's in.
Musicians appear to loud applause,
and the minstrel's tunes begin.
Dancers dance to the wild violins,
to mandolins, and Spanish guitars;
the drums beating frenzied rhythms,
beneath the moonlight and stars;
and the music flows, in a magical way,
at the house on the hill, near Golden Bay.

2
Both Michelangelo and Rembrandt
have paintings in each and every niche.
there is beauty everywhere you look.
An artistic masterpiece.
The walls and ceilings, overflowing,
with creations by the Old Masters.
Renoir, Cezanne and Degas too,
spread from the floor to rafter.
You can see it all, if you decide to stay,
at the house on the hill, near Golden Bay.

3
Majestic deer herds roam the meadows,
where peacock and pheasant strut around.
A forest; the picturesque backdrop;
above snow capped peaks abound
Swans gracefully glide on the river,
Waterfalls; where salmon swim, and leap.
An idyllic vision to cherish,
a memory to keep.
Where down by the sea, the dolphins dive and play
at the house on the hill, near Golden Bay.

4
The cinema shows the best movies,
by directors of the silver screen.
The top photographic imagery,
is waiting there to be seen.
A library of fact and fiction,
every meaningful word, that's been penned:
the list goes on and on forever,
perfection to the end.
Or relax in the sun, that shines everyday,
at the house on the hill, near Golden Bay

` **

Published in "Dancing till dawn broke"
By Parkinson's Disease Society
ISBN 0 - 9530233 0-3
` **

London Streets
© **Gordon martin**

It's dark and all tourists are at the movies or live shows,
and this is not the busy streets, it's the back roads visitors don't go.
I stumble over something laying heavy on the ground
and there's suddenly a tirade of abusive ranting sound.
I'm about to show a reaction when a face comes into view,
It's a boy no more than ten years old, with hair that's spiky blue.
He's a runaway, he's frightened and he's sleeping on the street,
I give him a pound and turn away, and he's already back asleep.
I pass a postcard stand and I admire the kids for having a go
at making an honest living, then suddenly two heavies make a show.
The stand is wrecked the postcards thrown and scattered everywhere
the owners, two girls are in tears, one has her head pulled back by her
hair.
The heavy that is holding it, pushes a finger to her nose
"You ask permission, first" he threatens, then jumps in a car and goes.
Down the road, a little further, there's a tramp rooting through a bin
And in a shady, well hid doorway, a man is pushing a needle into his
skin.
At Kings Cross, the ladies of the night, some pretty, but some ugly
too,
are strutting around trying to make a few pound, while their pimps
keep out of view,
Inside at the telephone kiosks, all filled with rows and rows of kids
who are ringing home and trying to explain why they did the things
they did.
The policemen look at you with suspicious, querying eyes,
but they've got so many things to sort, it comes as no surprise,
that unless you're violent, weird, aggressive or just ill
there really isn't a reaction from the lads in blue of the old bill
In a matter of hours you could go from being
a respected man, the type you'd like to meet,
to being just another number, and that's thousands, of down and
outs,
that people avoid when walking London's streets.

MANCHESTER UNITED
© **Gordon martin**

Take me down to a football pitch,
teach me how to run and play.
Nurture the skill of how to thrill
and who knows, some future day,
I'll walk upon that field of green,
by sixty thousand fans be seen,
Old Trafford the elusive dream,
to be one of that famous footballing team.

To play the game, to make a claim
of eternal and immortal fame.
Admired by peers, from far and wide,
as onward rolls the relentless tide.
England, Europe, then the World,
United banners everywhere unfurled.
Just to wear that blood red shirt with pride,
of the greatest and most loved club side.

SAME PAGE
© **Gordon martin**

1
The night's are drawing in again
A cold chill in the morning air
And a watery sun in the afternoon sky
The falling leaves lay everywhere
2
There's a heart beating for a lover
who's now in another time and place
where the sun is warm and it's barely dawn
and who now looks upon a different face
3
The letters screwed up on the floor
like the snow that's bound to come
empty words rescinded or forgotten
who sent what to where and when to whom
4
The slowly coming of a new age
the fast retreating of the old
like a tide life brings and takes away things
we cannot hope to own or hold
5
I'll sit with you sweet lady
the handsome man said to the one
that he now held in his arms so powerful
and we'll take a drink before you're gone
6
But be he the one whose heart beat
on that cold autumnal day
or the one reborn on the hot bright morn
it didn't matter either way
7
And if that embrace was only
a recollection of another place and age
or the magic somehow happening here and now
time would make them the same page

SOME PEOPLE
© Gordon martin

1
Some people need pleasure
some people need pain
some people need fruit
some people need grain
some people need detention
somehow we all know that's true
some people need attention
some people like you

2
Some friends need solitude
some friends need a crowd
some friends need to be quiet
some friends need to be loud
some friends need a direction
some don't know what to do
some friends lead from the front line
some friends just like you

3
Some partners need controlling
some partners need to be led
some partners will follow
some partners ahead
some partners need to be raising
some standards it's true
some partners need praising
some partners like you

4
Some families need occupation
some families need a good rest
some families will help out
some families are best
some families would walk barefoot
some million miles just for you
some family ties will never be cut
some families like you

VENICE
© **Gordon martin**

1
Remember walking through the alleyways
That shaded the burning sun
How they opened into piazzas
Where the children play and run
We sat drinking in that restaurant bar
And watched the world go by
Underneath an Italian sun
In an Italian azure sky
The city was so beautiful
Picturesque in every way
I'm going back again someday

2
The canals that formed a network
For the city buildings to stand upon
Where gondolas, carrying lovers
On calm waters glide upon
Being serenaded by the music
From the bands playing on the bridges
And swallows skimmed the water
Then flew up to the ridges
Painters painting pictures
As we walked along the way
I'm going back again someday

3
It's no wonder Goya painted masterpieces
Or that Italy has the finest art
So much beauty all around you
Where would you make a start
And though it's stood for ages
And is as pretty as it's unique
Each corner that you turn
Presents another view to keep
And hold ever in your memory
And makes you promise on going away
I'm going back again someday

SAN PEDRO
© Gordon martin

1
It's another hot summer morning
There's little noise from anywhere
A few birds call out to one another
Church bells ringing out somewhere
In the distance

2
Time is temporarily frozen
When nothing moves or makes a plan
An old man sits by a broken doorway
Beside a whirring squeaking fan
That can't cool him

3
A dog laying by his feet
Too lazy to catch a rat
Little use as a companion
Never even seen a cat
Hangs his tongue out

4
The dust track that meanders
Past the barrel by the door
Devoid of any cooling fresh rainwater
It's been dry two months or more
Has no purpose

5
For there is nowhere else to go to
On this hot sierra plain
If you don't quietly accept it
You'll simply go insane
Or die of heatstroke

6

And there are twenty, thirty, forty,
Fifty, sixty or even more
Replicas of this bland scenario
Where nothing changes anymore
This is San Pedro....

7
.........I was sitting in my garden
Browsing through the holiday mags
When I spotted the perfect getaway
So I'm packing up my bags
I've booked San Pedro

LIFE
© Gordon martin

1

When I was young and carefree
And thought life continued endlessly
And I could do just as I wanted
I worked and played so tirelessly

2

I thought I'll wait until tomorrow
It doesn't need to be today
Even then the old folk tried to tell me
That life didn't work that way

3

There's a promise that's been broken
There's a story not been told
There's a future in the balance
There's a soul already sold

4

I've got time enough to do things
I said, with the wisdom of a fool
I never realised that learning
Starts outside not inside the school

5

That the world is there before you
And what you see is what you get
And mistakes can't be corrected
And that your life is already set

6

There's a prison in the valley
There's a burning crackling fire

There's a hope of a new tomorrow
There's an aching, deep desire

7
So heed these words I tell you
Make the best of every day
Don't treat work as a religion
Find time to rest and play

8
No-one knows the setting of their life
Whether it's short or whether it's long
Whether it's happy or unfortunate
Whether it's right or whether it's wrong

9
There's a howling beast inside you
There's a longing to be free
There's a raging deep impatience
There's a resignation of what's to be

No Time
© Gordon martin

1
You've got time to shop for new clothes
You've got time to try on shoes
You've got time to listen to the radio
Or the television news
You've got time to play the lottery
You've got time to make a claim
So how come you ain't got time to say
I love you
And my name

2
You've got time to watch a talk show
You've got time to see a soap
You've got time to hear about the latest scam
Or else snort a line of dope
You've got time to phone a good friend
You've got time to play the game
So how come you ain't got time to say
I love you
And my name

3
You've got time to call beauticians
You've got time to cut your hair
You've got time enough to be omnipotent
Babe you're simply everywhere
You've got time to bless a poor man
You've got time to heal the lame
So how come you ain't got time to say
I love you
And my name

4
You've got time for taking holidays

You've got time for gardening too
You've got time to climb Mount Everest
Something that I wouldn't do
You've got time to wait for Oberammergau
You've got time to shoot for fame
So how come you ain't got time to say
I love you
And my name

5
You've got time for reading war and peace
You've got time to sing the blues
You've got time to talk to everyone
All the gossip that accrues
You've got time to watch the latest race
You've got time for laying blame
So how come you ain't got time to say
I love you
And my name

You Know
© Gordon martin

1
When you find that nothing of good seems to stay
When your dreams are shipwrecked on the reality of today
When you wonder what else you could possibly say
Look my way

2
When you're down and looking for a way to rise
When the world hits you with surprise after surprise
When you've had enough of emotions in disguise
Watch my eyes

3
I'll be there to see you through
I'll be there to do whatever I can do
I'll be waiting for a call from you

4
When you're tired of all the sweet talking freaks
When everything you have is broken or it leaks
When you shout quiet and everybody speaks
Don't wait weeks

5
When there's no harmony in anything you see
When things turn out some way it couldn't be
When all you want is a place you can be free
Look to me

6
I'll show you where to go
I'll help you make love grow
You know....
You know...

It's Over
© Gordon martin

Daylight finally pushed back the obstinate dark

that left you feeling as if no-one cared

and disguised and distorted everything

that we had collected together but would no longer share

The grey mist hung like an innocent victim

strung and swaying from the tallest oak tree

sad faces look down at a desolate patch

a man prays as he kneels on one knee

Who knows? Is it me they're saying good-bye to?

or am I again holding back a sad tear

on this morning that wears its despondency

like a cloak spread over all standing here

There's a babe in arms that cries for salvation

there an old flame shuffling cold feet in the crowd

There's a son or a mother relentlessly weeping

and the ones that loved me now cry out aloud

Tears of confusion, bitterness and injustice

mix with complete disbelief fuelled by rage
but don't cry, my sweet love, I'm not in the casket

That was just a vehicle I used to travel life's page.

I was here before evolution or creation

I'll be here if the Earth ceased to exist

and I carry two things that are forever treasured

Every time that you smiled and every time that we kissed

So go from this place of distorted confusion

there's nothing here for you to worry about

I'm safe now …

….and one day we'll be together

And happy and peaceful, of that I've no doubt.

Be cheerful! That's all I would want for you

I'm rid of the chains that once shackled me

You played the lament that I asked you to play

I am at peace now …..

…….and finally free

Tributes To Gordon
From His Memorial Service

The 'Manaia' is the Maori symbol for the
Spiritual Guardian guiding your spirit to where it is supposed to go when your time
comes.

To my very, very special Uncle Gordon

Now you're in a special place where you can
play your practical jokes on Granddad, argue
about football with Uncle Roy, and be free
of the chains that once shackled you.
Thank you for your patience and passion that
helped to guide me down the right road in life.
Thank you for caring.
'May you stay Forever Young'..............
Joy xxx & Jonathan

FOR MY UNCLE GORDON

Here's a small handful of cool things that you did for me when I was
young…

Taking me to see Wolverhampton Wanderers
Teaching me a few tricks about snooker and tennis
Playing me some inspirational music by Bob (especially good!)
Showing me how to win at space invaders

Small things to some people, but pretty big when you're a small kid.

Thanks for those and all the other things you taught me, shared with
me, helped me with, and especially, joked about.

Despite all the trials that were thrown at you, you managed to rise
above them all and smile.

In your own ever so dry, intelligent and sometimes poetic way you
brought a great deal of humour to just about all of the people you
met along the way.

Somebody once said that the most wasted day of all is one in which
we have not laughed. Based on that reckoning I don't think you
wasted too many.
I know despite the sorrow for all of us who love you, you have moved
on to a better place, and that somewhere wherever you are, I know
you'll be having a laugh in good company.

Sending you a piece of sunshine from the other side of the world.

All our love, Ian and Rowena

PS ………Now that you're up there, if you find that answer "blowing
in the wind" can you let me know what it is?

Tribute From Julia On Behalf Of Herself And Cathrine

My first sight of Gordon was when he arrived at our house as Aunty Maureen's boyfriend and suddenly this giant walked into our home! I must admit we were all a bit nervous as he was also Aunty Maureen's boss. I thought he looked very smart with his dark hair and his tash but I had never seen anyone so tall.

Me and our Cath sized him up a bit at first but it was not long before he tried to break the ice with us by drawing really good elephants, he made a rod for his own back there because we did not leave him alone that afternoon, he read us stories and drew loads more elephants and told us jokes. Cath even made him wear one of those 80s headbands which we called deelyboppers.

It wasn't long before the giant we first saw became our "Uncle Gordon". After he left our house my Mum said to my Dad "What do you think Tet?" My dad being a man of few words summed it up nicely. "Sound," he said. As weeks went by Gordon became a great Uncle to us and a great friend to my Mum and Dad. He was good fun and loved parties. He even became a superhero. At our Cath's birthday party, one of her friends asked who he was "It's my Uncle Gordon" she said to which her friend replied, "Oh, Flash Gordon". Flash Gordon became his name for quite a while.
It was not until I became a teenager that I really discovered how "cool" my Uncle Gordon really was. I really liked music then and I discovered his record collection; he had all the latest stuff and I was over the moon when he copied The Pet Shop Boys latest album for me.

As well as being a great joke teller and artist, there was a serious side to Gordon as he was also a very compassionate man. He provided great support to our family at sad times especially when we lost my Grandma and Mum.

As I grew older I could see Gordon was a very intelligent and talented man and I was greatly inspired by him when I decided to continue my education. I even chose the same course as him. He used to let me use his computer to type up my assignments. By this time Gordon was writing poetry which turned out to be another great talent of his, he would share some of his latest poems with me and give me advice on my assignments while Aunty Maureen made us cheese and tomato sandwiches.
Gordon also tried to make me a football fan although I never really knew whether his loyalties lay with Manchester United or Wolves, it seemed to be different depending on who he was talking to or how each team was doing at any given time!

Although Gordon may have changed over the years as he was fighting with Parkinson's he still remained a prolific poet, artist and songwriter. My children recently said he could draw the best Bart Simpsons in the world!!

Gordon still managed to keep his sense of humour too. One day when Cath went to visit him on respite, she gave him a kiss to say goodbye and when one of the nurses asked who she was, Gordon replied "I have no idea".

I'm sure we all have special memories of Gordon and we will all remember him for many different qualities, but I will remember him most for the sheer determination which he has shown throughout his life both in his professional work and later on when dealing with his illness. Gordon would say "Rules are meant to be broken" and he may have broken a few but it is better to live life to the full and take a few risks rather than have a life full of regrets.

From Derek

What did Gordon mean to me?

I looked up to him in more ways than one
........and he looked down at me.........
Since he was much taller than I am!

Though I am older than he by a few years he was like my big brother
and I admired him immensely.

Nothing was too much trouble and he would
do anything for me.....even in the condition
he was in......
"No problem Mate....sorted" he would say.

Gordon believed in quality and went through life
as though he was on a mission,
always looking ahead,
no time to talk about his illness,
only in his poetry, which was amazing to me.

I remember him telling me about an incident which took place in a
lift in America. A young boy entered the lift with him and asked if he
was going up to which Gordon replied yes. The boy studied him, as
the Parkinsons caused his head to shake to and fro and then said "So
why are you
shaking your head?" Gordon was highly amused.

He would ring me at the most inconvenient times,
mostly when I was watching the news,
just to tell me there was a better programme
on the other side, or to tell me a joke. I miss that now.

When you go to sleep and if you dream and if Gordon's in that dream
then it will be a nice dream,
as Gordon was such a very nice man.

As I left Gordon for the last time, I said Goodbye to him with a great sadness. Then in my heart I said to him "Gordon, you've left your wheelchair behind"
In my mind's eye he looked at me and grinned in his own inimitable way and replied,
"Don't need it mate.........Got wings!"